They Also Served

They Also Served

Wives of Civil War Generals

Robert Wilson & Carl Clair

To order additional copies of this book, contact:
Xlibris Corporation
1-888-795-4274
www.Xlibris.com
Orders@Xlibris.com
28810

CONTENTS

"We often hear the remark that these are days that try men's souls. I think they try women's souls, too. I shall remember you and all the noble women of the North when this land is at peace."

Abraham Lincoln

"I know also that the story of the War Between the States will never be fully and fairly written if the achievements of women are left untold."

Fletcher Green
"Women of the Confederacy in War Time".

Introduction

Celebrating his first night in the President's House, John Adams offered the following toast, "May none but honest and wise men ever rule under this house." To which his wife Abigail replied, "Remember the ladies."

It is hoped that this modest work, which we have entitled "*They Also Served*", will shed new light on the lives of the remarkable women who shared the history of this terrible time along with their warrior husbands. We have gathered these stories from various sources including books, magazines, the Internet, and several archival collections. A conscientious effort has been made to insure the information used in the telling of these stories has not only been accurate, but also fully documented.

After Fort Sumter, the men left in droves obeying the call of their governments to serve with the armies being formed, not to return for years or at all. The glamorous picture of the brave men riding off to war is a popular one, however, it remained for the wives to take up the many burdens their departures left behind. Overnight, wives became heads of family with sole responsibility for maintaining home and hearth. Most were completely unschooled in managing household finances or supervising plantation or farm laborers. Alone, they bore the deaths of their children and suffered the shock of news from the front that their husbands had been killed or captured. Somehow, most of them survived and, in the process, added poignant, and truly amazing stories to Civil War folklore.

They managed the home front as single parents for years. They followed their husbands to the front providing comfort and support, displaying great courage under dangerous and trying conditions. They provided badly needed nursing care. They developed skill at unraveling the politics of the military bureaucracy seeking ways they might support the careers of their loved ones. They suffered the anguish of spousal unfaithfulness. They served and died in support of a conflict that they little understood. Throughout the long four years they remained faithful to their respective causes without complaint and, often, with good cheer.

One of our early favorites was the fascinating Fanny Haralson Gordon, wife of Confederate General John Brown Gordon. This formidable woman decided to remain with her husband as much of the time as possible under what, at times, became truly hazardous conditions. With the professional help of the staff at the University of Georgia Libraries we were able to develop a profile of Fanny's life prior to, during, and after the Civil War. Her spectacular story drove us forward with renewed energy. We next found the flamboyant Libby Custer, the noble and stoic Mary Custis Lee, followed by the melancholy Fanny Chamberlain. We were hooked.

Read on and enjoy. We hope what you learn here will also illuminate the lives of the generals involved by viewing them in their roles as husbands. Doing this work certainly enriched our appreciation.

The wives are presented by date of birth so Mary Custis Lee is first and Irene Rucker Sheridan is last.

Acknowledgements

Two books attracted out attention to the role of women in the Civil War. Eileen Conklin's *Women at Gettysburg 1863* published in 1993 and Mary Massey's *Women in the Civil War* which appeared in 1966. These authors called our attention to the vital role women played during these troubled times, a role, if mentioned at all, usually downplayed in most works on the War. Then, to our delight, Carol Bleser and Lesley Gordon's *Intimate Strategies of the Civil War* debuted in 2001 just about the time we were getting starting. This book helped us out big time; convincing us this was an important topic worth pursuing.

One always approaches literary endeavors on obscure subjects such as this one with a certain amount of caution and concern about what research materials will be available, where they are located, how accessible they are and how cooperative the "keepers" of these materials will be on the authors behalf. We have been very lucky here having discovered many resourceful "helpers" along the way who have given unselfishly of their time and knowledge towards bringing this work to fruition. Their enthusiasm and professionalism has made this project a rewarding one.

Very special kudos to Phyllis Schaffer for her skillful editing which illuminated obscure passages, guarded against the perils of overblown rhetoric, and purged much superfluous verbiage.

Janice Shepherd of Columbia, Maryland for her initial interest in the idea that the wives' stories should be told and for her input to many of the early stories.

Joseph Marshall Mathias provided us with the opportunity to use some stories that were published earlier in his American Legion newsletter, providing editorial help in the process.

The always-helpful Monocacy Battlefield Park Ranger, Gloria Swift, who showed us where to find many useful "nuggets."

Chuck Barber and the staff at Hargrett Rare Book and Manuscript Library at the University of Georgia Library for their cheerful and expert help in obtaining vital material not available elsewhere.

Toni Carter and Jeffrey Ruggles of the Virginia Historical Society in Richmond made time spent there most rewarding.

Dan Peterson, the great grandson of James and Louise Longstreet, for his reactions to and encouragement of this project and for the photos of Louise.

Cinnamon Catlin-Legutko, director of the General Lew Wallace Study and Museum who not only provided us with much useful information but passed us on to several other lucrative sources.

Gail Stephens of the William H. Smith Library at the Indiana Historical Society who led us to helpful material.

Richard Sommers of the U.S. Army Military History Institute at Carlisle Barracks, Pennsylvania offered many helpful suggestions in our search for data on the wives. The entire staff at Carlisle was just great.

Patricia Wood at the Pickett Society helped clarify some confusion on Sallie Pickett's name.

Al Wertman a.k.a. General Jubal Early helped with information about Julia McNealey.

Phyllis Vannoy Spiker, archivist at the University of Kentucky Martin Luther King Library identified important information for us.

The McKeldin Library at the University of Maryland College Park let us take out numerous vital books with very generous time allowances.

Joanne Arbuckle was a willing and effective "web-researcher."

Finally, and with great sincerity, the authors wish to thank the many family members and friends who have shown great forbearance while we were preoccupied with "Wives". They tolerated our obsession while providing encouragement along with many cogent and thoughtful suggestions; all of which much improved the work at hand.

Robert Wilson
Wilsonm121@comcast.net

Carl Clair
cclair@comcast.net

Mary Custis Lee

First President's Great-Granddaughter

When Lieutenant Robert E. Lee married Mary Anna Randolph Custis, the bride's pedigree far surpassed his own modest and somewhat troubled lineage. Born on Oct 1, 1808, Mary Custis was heiress to the most storied heritage in America. She was the great granddaughter of Martha Washington and the daughter of the first president's adopted son, George Washington Custis. Along with this impressive genealogy, she was also an essential part of the landed gentry of Northern Virginia. Her father had inherited over 50,000 acres of Virginia plantation land in five locations, including the 1,100 acres at Arlington with its majestic view of the nation's capitol across the Potomac River. The inheritance also included more than 100 slaves and a large sum of money. She grew up amid this affluence as an only child. Three of her siblings had died in infancy. Her upbringing included all the fineries that privilege had to offer—the finest tutors, numerous trips to wealthy relatives, a distinguished library, and sophisticated playmates.

Her childhood days were filled with tutoring sessions, prayer, bible studies, art lessons, gardening, and some play. She learned to read Latin, Greek, and French. Her French was so good that when ordering Victor Hugo's *Les Miserables*, she told the dealer to send it along in either French or English. Her father was committed to collecting George Washington's papers and other objects of historical significance such as his swords and other military paraphernalia. She was thus exposed to the role her family had played in history and this, in turn, stimulated her own deep interest in the past.

Mary matured into a delicate southern belle. Although not renowned for her beauty and often troubled by serious bouts of ill health, she had a fine mind, charming demeanor, a quick wit, excellent manners, and superior skills as a conversationalist. Her sterling family background, her affluence, and her personal attributes combined to make her much sought after in the Northern Virginia-Washington social circles. One of her earliest courtiers was the 32-year-old Congressman from Texas, Sam Houston who made several trips to Arlington to plead his cause. But Mary's eyes roamed elsewhere and when Robert came home from West Point in his uniform, her heart was in jeopardy.

The son of Revolutionary War cavalry leader "Light Horse Harry" Lee and Ann Carter, Robert was only two years old when his father was jailed for debt. Four years later in 1813, the senior Lee sailed for the Caribbean seeking to avoid his creditors and hoping to restore his health, to no avail. He returned to America in 1818 and died of cancer on March 24. Ann Lee was left with the difficult task of acting as a single parent to her children. She taught them piety and discipline and made sure Robert remembered his father as a war hero.

As the relationship between Mary and Robert deepened, Mary was also experiencing a newfound zeal and commitment to Christianity, an epiphany that lasted her lifetime. She fretted that Robert's faith was superficial and incomplete. Her letters to him were filled with exuberance toward her new found faith and she even began to doubt whether his lack of religious enthusiasm would preclude their marriage. However, love prevailed over religious scruples. On his next leave the two spent a long and lovely day together and when Robert proposed, her answer was prompt and definite, "Yes, Robert, yes!!"

The wedding took place on June 30, 1831. Mary's parents made sure that it would be a wedding to remember. The house was finely decorated and ablaze with lights. Mary was dressed elegantly but in the tasteful style expected of her. The party lasted for several days before the newlyweds accompanied by Mary's mother left to visit relatives. Lt. Lee had come a long way from the genteel poverty of his youth to being married to the "mistress of Arlington."

When Robert was preparing to leave for his new post at Fort Monroe, Virginia, Mary was eager to accompany him although she had a difficult time leaving her mother. Mrs. Custis wrote to her daughter that she would do her best to be happy without her. Mary needed to make many adjustments as she transitioned from living at Arlington with its many servants and domestic refinements to a two-room officer's quarters with dirt floors.

When the Lees returned home for the Christmas holidays, Mary learned that she was pregnant and Robert returned to Fortress Monroe alone. George Washington Custis Lee (Boo) was born on September 16, 1832. The Lees went on to have seven children in all, four daughters and three sons between 1832 and 1846. Two of the daughters died young, and all of the boys served as officers during the Civil War. Mary was a lax disciplinarian and Robert often admonished her about keeping the children under control.

In one letter he urged her to exercise firm authority while avoiding severity or strictness. Instructions such as these established a precedent that was to plague their relationship throughout the early years of their marriage. While he was away for prolonged periods before and during the war, he consistently proffered advice on how she, alone, was to raise their offspring. In this regard, he could be a difficult mate.

In thirty-nine years of marriage she lived in numerous places from Virginia to Missouri from West Point, New York to Baltimore and finally, Lexington, Virginia. She made a valiant effort adjusting to the many adverse conditions she faced but was always relieved and happy to return home to Arlington.

Both she and Robert opposed secession. She thought that the other southern states might have left South Carolina alone. She felt that so isolated, they would have suffered badly and eventually rejoined the Union. Further, she thought that the public should give more attention to the memory and precepts of George Washington and in so doing would not be so ripe for disunion.

Like more than a few upper class southerners, the Lees had a strong moral aversion to slavery but could not work out how the southern way of life would function should the slaves be freed. Mary's parents and grandparents had also experienced this dilemma where slavery was viewed as a curse inherited from their ancestors who had made slavery an economic necessity.

As Robert was enhancing his military reputation with his performance during the war with Mexico, Mary had her first long-term experience at being in charge at Arlington. From all accounts she faced the challenge with fortitude and did quite well raising the children, handling the finances, entertaining guests and managing the plantation.

In 1852 Robert was assigned to West Point as commandant, and Mary and the children soon joined him. She was comfortable there with both the living accommodations and the easy access to Arlington if she was needed. At West Point it was common for many guests to appear for dinner at a moments notice. Mary and the cook learned how to make "thin soup," a dish that permitted stretching the available larder to make sure there was enough for all. She handled everyone so graciously that the "thinnest" of the soup was overlooked.

In 1859 Mary completed her book on the lives of George Washington and George Washington Custis; a work of love and gratitude. She also completed her father's bibliography on George Washington. Her literary endeavors received favorable reviews and enjoyed good sales in America and overseas.

When Virginia seceded, Robert, with Mary's consent, resigned his commission from the U. S. Army and joined the Confederacy. The Lees immediate concern was the fate of Mary's home precariously situated just over the Potomac River from the Yankee capitol. Word soon arrived that the Federals were determined to take over Arlington and that she should, very quickly, save what she could and move on. She buried some things and took other valuables with her. The Union troops occupied Arlington on May 23, 1861: her beloved ancestral home was in enemy hands. Mary was never to live there again.

When she got word that Arlington was being mistreated, she complained to Union General Irvin McDowell who assured her that the house and grounds would not be greatly disturbed; a promise impossible to honor. The trees and fences were dismantled and used for firewood, the house itself was used as a Union hospital, and the dead were buried in Mary's rose garden. Faced with these wanton acts of war, Mary's views towards the North hardened and she predicted that the South would resist fiercely.

During the war Mary, in spite of her fragile physical condition, was called upon numerous times to nurse the ill and the wounded, either in her home, the home of others, or at Richmond hospitals. One of her patients was her own son, Rooney, who was being cared for at Hickory Hill just north of Richmond when Union forces entered the house and took him into custody. They curtly informed the distraught mother that since they couldn't capture Robert, this Lee would have to do.

When the Confederates abandoned Richmond, Mary decided to stay and take her chances. This proved a wise move as General Grant ordered guards to protect her and her house. The professed Yankee hater was grateful for this act of benevolence and reciprocated by preparing food for Union guards.

On Saturday, April 15, Mary heard a commotion at the door and looked up to see Robert and their son Rooney entering the house. The war was over. Her husband and one of her sons had come home. Robert's appearance caused Mary great concern—he was much heavier with a completely gray beard and had some difficultly walking due to shortness of breath caused by angina. He was unemployed, and his holdings of $20,000 were in worthless Confederate bonds. He had no job, no income, and no home, yet, the future beckoned.

Away West in the Shenandoah Valley, the Board of Trustees of a small college was meeting and Robert's fate was being discussed. Would General Lee be willing to take on the task of rebuilding a small provincial college? He accepted and became the President of Washington College in Lexington, soon to be renamed Washington and Lee. The salary was a meager $1,500 a year but the Lees could manage. The trustees built the new president a home on campus and Robert and Mary settled in. They became a vital part of the school and invited students and faculty in for social evenings. By this time Mary was wheelchair bound, but was always ready to greet her guests. Robert insisted on being the one to wheel Mary around the large front porch, claiming it was "his privilege"; she must have basked in the attention. For the aging warrior, a second career had begun.

When their son Custis received an appointment at Virginia Military Academy, which adjoins the campus of Washington & Lee, Mary was pleased to have her family close by.

Concerned about Mary's welfare in the event of Robert's death, the trustees offered her the use of the home on campus rent free for life. They also granted her a pension. Robert protested that this money should be used to benefit the students; they acknowledged his views but went ahead with their plans.

Robert was very successful at raising funds for the college and had a chapel built on the campus, which was posthumously named after him. When completed, he occupied space in the basement for his office. Later, he and members of his family were entombed there.

When General Lee died in 1870, Mary was unable to attend the funeral services due to her increasing ill health. Custis replaced his father as President of Washington and Lee and lived in the house with his family and Mary until she died.

In early summer of 1873, Mary felt drawn to return one last time to her beloved Arlington. With the help of many, she made the long and painful trip. She recalled nostalgically, "I rode out to my dear old home, so changed it seemed but as a dream of the past. I could not have realized it was Arlington but for the few old oaks that had been spared, & the trees planted on the lawn by the Gen'l & myself which are raising their tall branches to Heaven which seems to smile on the desecration around them."

Mary died in November 1873 and is buried next to Robert in the chapel vault.

In her loving biography of Mary Lee, Kimberly Largent concluded, "She was actually a courageous, selfless, creative woman who managed to solely, for the most part, raise seven children while battling many physical ailments." She added, "Always suffering from constant pain, she went about her life with an unwavering faith in God . . ."

Confederate General Robert E. Lee is among the best-known generals in American history. He gained military distinction in the Mexican War and was offered command of all Union forces at the start of the Civil War, but declined due to his stated loyalty to his home state of Virginia. For two years he was successful in consistently defeating Union forces. Eventually, Union superiority in both men and resources led to his defeat. After the war he became president of Washington College in Lexington, Virginia where he died in 1870.

Eliza Clinch Anderson

"I must take Sgt. Hart to Robert"

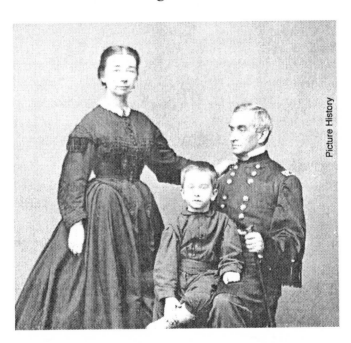

Eliza Clinch and Robert Anderson were both southern born. Eliza's father, Duncan Clinch, was a lieutenant colonel in the U.S. Infantry and fought in the War of 1812 and the Mexican War. He owned a plantation in Georgia and served one term in Congress. Robert was born in Louisville, Kentucky in 1805. He served his country well in all her wars from the Black Hawk to the Civil War and was in command of the Union forces at Fort Sumter in 1860.

From the time that South Carolina seceded from the United States on December 20, 1860, Fort Sumter was destined to play a crucial role in the ultimate descent to war. Located well out in Charleston Harbor, the continued Union occupation of the fort was considered an insult to Southern sovereignty. As Elisa Anderson read the headlines describing the tense situation, she pondered the fate of her husband and his troops and considered ways in which she might help. Concern for a loved one assumed to be in harm's way, often precipitates strange and unusual thoughts and actions. On the night of December 26, 1861 she had reached a resolution that the one person who could provide her beleaguered husband with badly needed assistance was his former sergeant, Peter Hart. He had been with Robert at three of his last four posts and was considered highly reliable. But first, she needed to find this dedicated Irishman.

Armed with a New York City directory, she started her door-to-door search. When her first day's efforts failed, she continued into a second day. Down to her last three "Peter Harts," she found someone who thought there was a person by that name on the police force. Eliza contacted the police superintendent's office that put her in touch with the long sought sergeant.

"Please come at once", she wrote, "this is urgent." Peter and his wife arrived soon thereafter. "I need your husband's help" Eliza told the supportive Mrs. Hart, who replied, "He'll do his level best, Mistress."

She then outlined her plan asking Peter to accompany her to Charleston and then out to Fort Sumter so he could be with her husband during the troubled times ahead. After a quick glance at his wife who nodded approval, Hart replied, "I will do anything for you. When do we leave?" She replied that they would leave at 6 o'clock the next morning.

Eliza told no one but her nurse that she was leaving. She asked the nurse to care for the children and swore her to secrecy. She was certain that both her family and her physician would disapprove of such a difficult trip.

The next morning she and Peter boarded a train for Charleston. There, her request for a carriage with which to continue their journey was denied. She wrote a note to her friend South Carolina Governor Francis Pickens. Quickly, without the Governor's intervention, a carriage was made available that took the two travelers to the Old Mill House where her brother Bayard was staying. He was shocked yet delighted to see Eliza.

Her mission made clear, Bayard accompanied her to the Governor who, while willing to give her a pass, had some misgivings about Sgt. Hart. She pleaded; he relented and even gave her a bundle of letters for the soldiers at Fort Sumter. Together, the two were rowed out to the Fort on the final leg of their strange journey.

"I have brought you Peter Hart!" she exclaimed to her surprised husband. He was shocked yet pleased to see her. He took Eliza to his quarters and served her some nourishment. However, her pass was good for only one hour, so, leaving Robert and Sgt. Hart behind, she returned to Charleston.

Bayard and his friends in Charleston offered her food and lodging for as long as she wished. Determined to return to her children, however, she departed on the evening train for Washington. Her brother arranged for a bed to be placed on the train but in spite of these precautions, she was nearly unconscious when she arrived back in Washington. A room was found for her in the Willard Hotel where she recuperated for several days before returning to New York.

Peter Hart's presence did nothing to change the outcome of the subsequent Confederate siege of Fort Sumter. But Eliza was able to derive great comfort knowing that Robert had Peter Hart at his side while the shelling and eventual surrender of the Fort took place. When Anderson's soldiers arrived in New York, Eliza and the children along with an enthusiastic crowd were there to greet them. They were being honored as war heroes, the first Union soldiers to see action in the Civil War.

And so Eliza's strange mission had been accomplished. Alone, and against great odds, with no federal government assistance, she had acted with courage and resolve to try to help her husband during a time of crisis.

Robert retired from the Army in 1863 due to illness. Abraham Lincoln asked him to return to Fort Sumter on April 14, 1865 to raise the United States flag on the fourth anniversary of the surrender. General Anderson was unable to pass on his impressions of this ceremonial event to the President since he had been assassinated on April 14.

After the war, Eliza and Robert went to Europe in hopes of improving his health, but he died in France in 1871 and was buried at West Point.

Major Robert Anderson was the commander of Union troops stationed at Fort Sumter in Charleston, South Carolina on the eve of the Civil War. His army service was, for the most part, prior to the Civil War. During the war he served briefly as a general in Kentucky. On the fourth anniversary of the surrender, he attended the raising of the U.S. flag at Fort Sumter as personal representative of the President.

Lizinka Campbell Ewell

"Petticoat Government"

Courtesy Donald C Pfanz

Lizinka Campbell Brown brought an intriguing and unique background to her marriage to Confederate General Richard Ewell. Daughter of Harriet Stoddert and George Washington Campbell, her father was a prominent antebellum Tennessee planter who served three terms in the U. S. Congress, along with being Secretary of the Treasury and as President James Monroe's ambassador to Russia. Shortly after the family arrived in St. Petersburg in 1818, a typhus epidemic swept through the city taking the lives of all three of their children.

Lizinka was born in St. Petersburg on February 24, 1820, was named Elizabeth McKay but was always called Lizinka in honor of Czar Alexander's wife the Empress Lizinka.

The family returned to Nashville where she received a privileged education that included proficiency on the piano and harp as well as fluency in French and Italian. In 1832, President Andrew Jackson appointed Campbell as a commissioner to settle claims with France. In this capacity, the family moved to Washington where as a young teenager Lizinka enjoyed the social life of the nation's capitol. Her looks, charm, and her father's wealth drew many admirers including her cousin Richard Ewell who was sufficiently enchanted to propose marriage. She declined, and in 1839 she married James Percy Brown. Ewell resigned himself to bachelorhood.

Brown proved to be an abnormally cruel and sadistic spouse who derived delight in tormenting Lizinka with details of his extramarital sexual conquests. Returning from a trip to Mississippi, he tauntingly asked how she would feel if he told her that he had impregnated a mutual friend. Her pain and torment ended in 1844 when Brown committed suicide leaving her with three small children. Brown sought to inflict one final cruelty by writing his wife out of his will and leaving his considerable wealth to his sons. Lizinka fought this arrangement and, overcoming considerably social prejudice, finally had the will annulled in her favor, thus adding to the already massive fortune inherited from her father (15,000 acres of land and an estimated $20,000) she became Tennessee's most eligible heiress with assets estimated at $500,000 in 1854.

Nineteen years elapsed from Brown's death until Lizinka married General Ewell. They were formative years and provide some keen insights into her evolving personality. Embittered by her disastrous first marriage and the long legal struggle to claim her rights to Percy Brown's estate, she turned her energy to raising her children and managing her vast plantation holdings. She learned from experience to compete and survive in what was exclusively a man's world. She developed a deep distrust of men in general and came to rely on her own business acumen and decision making ability. Deeply etched memories of her first marriage made any thoughts of remarriage a dim prospect. Savoring her autonomy and independence, the thought of subordinating either of these precious and hard won aspects of her personality to any man had little appeal to this successful and determined woman. Interestingly, she did offer cousin Richard an opportunity to manage one of her plantations. Although the offer was appealing, he did not accept it.

When the U. S. Army surrender at Fort Sumter finally turned into the Civil War, Lizinka and Ewell were once again united. She had come to Virginia to be with her son, Campbell Brown, who had a position on Ewell's staff. He was delighted to see her and staged a brigade review in her honor. The cousins announced their engagement in December 1861. This shift in Lizinka's attitude toward men appears to have been motivated by sincere feelings for Ewell, but it is also conceivable that by making this commitment she was also ensuring that her fiancée could keep her son out of harm's way. From back home in Nashville, Likinka wrote Ewell affectionate letters stimulating him to envisage a bright future together. To this end he wrote, " . . . it seems to me that the future has more to look forward to than I ever thought possible."

When General U. S. Grant's 1862 spring campaign led to the fall of Forts Henry and Donelson thus opening up central Tennessee to invasion, Confederate troops abandoned Nashville and retreated south. Before fleeing, Lizinka transferred title to her property to Unionist friends hoping to avoid confiscation by advancing Federal troops. She also wrote pleading letters to Grant and General Don Carlos Buell asking them to protect her house—to no avail. Union soldiers seized the house and turned it over to the military governor of Tennessee, Andrew Johnson, who used it as his residence for the next three years. Lizinka's Spring Hill plantation suffered a much worse fate when Federal troops seized 10,000 pounds of bacon, burned the barn, and stole all the livestock.

On August 28, as Ewell was attempting to get a clearer view of ongoing infantry operations at Groveton Crossing during the second battle of Bull Run, a Yankee bullet destroyed his left kneecap. The leg subsequently required amputation placing him out of combat for the next nine months and eventually leading to a marked change in his military performance.

By mid-September, he was reunited with Lizinka. She came to oversee his recovery, to reinvigorate their courtship, and to agree to marry him the following May. His infatuation with his lovely cousin, which had sustained him through almost three decades as a bachelor, finally bore fruit.

Biographers have reflected on General Ewell's curious tendency to periodically hallucinate that he was a bird. He would chirp softly in his tent for hours at a time, accepting only sunflower seed or grains of wheat at mealtimes. His big, hawkish nose and impressive bald dome made him look like a feathered creature, complimenting this birdlike behavior.

It had been General Stonewall Jackson's deathbed wish that Richard Ewell replace him as commander of the Second Corps. General Robert E. Lee concurred and, on May 23, Ewell was promoted to Lieutenant General thus becoming the third ranking officer in the Confederate Army. Three days later Ewell and Lizinka were married and shortly thereafter, the groom was ordered to Fredericksburg— the Army of Northern Virginia was moving north. But circumstances had changed since his last command—he had lost a leg and he had been married. Some historians have suggested that these changes were detrimental to his former performance standards.

As the commander's wife, Lizinka felt that it was her role to be at her husband's side whenever possible. Her presence, however, generated much ill will among Ewell's staff. Domineering her husband was one thing but her efforts to extend this domination to the operation of the 2nd Corps created animosity all around. One member of Ewell's staff remarked: "She manages everything from the General's affairs down to the courier who carries his dispatches." This did much to stimulate rumors about "petticoat government."

She saw disloyalty everywhere and became convinced that several of her husband's subordinates were conspiring against him. Lizinka also attempted to control Ewell's behavior on the battlefield to keep him and her son Campbell Brown out of danger. One of Ewell's biographers sums it up this way: " . . . it was inevitable that he should put his trust in a strong but loving wife. Mrs. Ewell assumed her position for one simple reason: (he) was proud of his wife and not only seized every opportunity to show her off but also allowed, even encouraged, her to take the forefront."

Although he was medically cleared to return to duty from wounds sustained at Spotsylvania Court House, General Lee was convinced it was time for the 2nd Corps commander to go. On November 15, he ordered him relieved and put General Jubal Early in charge. Ewell had become a combat commander without a command. He followed Lee's army in retreat and was captured at Sayler's Creek several days prior to Appomattox.

He and Campbell Brown were imprisoned at Fort Warren in Boston. Lizinka, seeking their release, wrote a letter to the President's wife eliciting her sympathy as a mother in support of her cause. For unknown reasons this letter infuriated Andrew Johnson and he had her arrested. Shocked by this unexpected response, Lizinka was at wits end, unable to determine how to react or what to do next. She viewed this detainment as: " . . . a mystery & is beginning to have on my mind the evil affect of a ghost story—some unseen & dreadful because you cannot get hold of it." Eventually released, by mid-summer, she moved to Rhode Island to be near her loved ones until they were released in late July 1865.

Civilian life suited Ewell and he plunged into the management of Lizinka's plantation at Spring Hill. She expressed a strong desire to move to Nashville or Richmond where they could enjoy a more dynamic social life. He ignored her, continuing to immerse himself in farm management, turning Spring Hill into a prosperous stock farm. He frequently left her alone when he made business trips to Mississippi. Their relationship grew strained, as Ewell seemed to go out of his way to demonstrate his independence and overcome the dominance that Lizinka had imposed on him during the war years. He often made decisions in managing her holdings without consulting her. Things finally erupted in early 1870 when Lizinka got word that Ewell seemed to prefer being in Mississippi than with her at Spring Hill. This pushed her over the edge: "If you choose to stay at Melrose," she wrote, "and let business here go to the dogs do so, but . . . I'll just go somewhere else, where I can have peace & rest . . . I won't stay here. O how I hate it."

Ewell came home and the crisis was averted. He was proud of his accomplishments as a farmer. He had taken a war torn and rundown Tennessee farm and brought it back to prosperity in just three years.

In their late years, Richard and Lizinka grew to be very fond of their grandchildren, Hattie's four girls and Campbell's three boys. They drew pleasure in giving them gifts and seeing them romp around the plantation grounds. But Ewell was aging rapidly and the stress of his long work hours along with his war wounds had weakened his frail body. In January 1872 the weather turned nasty, "raw and damp." On Monday, January 8, he caught a chill and was eventually bedridden with what was diagnosed as pneumonia. Lizinka kept a constant sickbed vigil, a devotion that was to cost her life. She contracted "well developed acute pneumonia" and died on January 22, 1872. Ewell lingered on and when told of his wife's death, he became agitated, called for a locket containing her picture to be hung around his neck, which he put over his heart. He was to follow her three days later.

General Ewell and Lizinka are both buried in the Old City Cemetery in Nashville.

Lt. General Richard Ewell fought with distinction at First and Second Manassas, the Valley campaign of 1862 and the Seven Days. He lost a leg at the battle of Groveton. After Gettysburg, he was retired from field command. He lived out his life as a successful farmer on his wife's plantations. He died at Spring Hill, Tennessee where he died on January 25, 1872.

Margaretta Sergeant Meade

"Do not accept it"

Margeretta, who was always called Margaret, was born on June 26, 1814. She was the first daughter of Margaretta Watmough and John Sergeant. Her education was well attended to and Margaret subsequently developed a wide range of cultural interests including facility with four languages and proficiency at the piano.

Her mother died when she was young and Margaret served as hostess for her father who was a Pennsylvania politician and well known in Washington D.C. political circles. He served five terms in Congress and ran for vice president with Henry Clay in 1932. For some reason, John turned down offers for appointed positions. He declined to serve on the Supreme Court, in a cabinet position, and as the minister to England.

George Meade was the son of Margaret Coates Meade and Richard W. Meade. He was born in Spain in 1815 when his father was serving as an agent for the United States Navy. They had been a wealthy family, but his father lost most of his money as he worked for the cause of Spain during the Napoleonic wars. After attending West Point, George was assigned to duty in Florida where he became ill and eventually resigned from the Army. He returned north and went to Washington D.C. where he met Margaret. When the future Mrs. Meade set her eyes on George, she was impressed. Her father, however, had serious reservations; his other daughters had married into high Washington society and thought his first-born could do better. Eventually, he overcame his reservations and became fond of George.

Margaret and George were married December 31, 1840 in Washington, D.C. The wedding reception was held in Georgetown and was attended by many officers, both Army and Navy.

Margaret spent many months alone while George was on military assignments. Fortunately, she saved his many letters, but since he did not save hers, much of their relationship can only be inferred from the one source. It is clear that he was devoted to her and their children, three sons and four daughters. The family moved with him to his various military assignments when possible. His second son, George, also served in the Army and was his father's aide during the battle of Gettysburg.

Margaret received one letter in which her husband got a bit carried away with his description of the Mexican *senioritas* who were helping him with his Spanish lessons. He went on to detail how their manner of dress would make eastern girls blush. One can imagine Margaret's reaction. She was raising three children alone, and was not likely to appreciate her spouse cavorting with the local lovelies. Whatever her response, the *senioritas* were never mentioned again.

When the Civil War started, George was a captain stationed near Lake Superior. Using her family's political influence, Margaret did what she could to seek his advancement. She probably didn't need to push too hard, for he had earned a fine reputation in the Mexican War and was soon commissioned as a brigadier general.

In the Seven Days Battle in 1862, George received two serious wounds and while awaiting transport home to a Philadelphia hospital, he wrote to Margaret that his wounds were not life threatening. Margaret and their son Sergeant met the ship and went aboard to greet George. The *Philadelphia Press* ran a story on the convalescing warrior that greatly enhanced his reputation.

After the Battle of Chancellorsville, President Lincoln offered George command of the Army of the Potomac. Margaret, who was in D.C. at the time, reacted to this news with vigor and urgency: "Do not accept it!" She was convinced that it would ruin his career. While agreeing with her that command of the Army was more likely to destroy a reputation than enhance it, he listened to his own council and took the job.

Margaret received numerous letters from George during and after the Battle of Gettysburg. These letters offer powerful insights into his thinking about the mighty conflict he was engaged in and generally ended with admonitions seeking her prayers that would permit him to continue to serve his country in this noble cause. After his fine performance at Gettysburg, the Philadelphia newspapers ran huge headlines honoring their local hero.

Margaret became upset when some newspapers expressed support for opinions that General Meade should have pursued General Robert E. Lee with more vigor after Gettysburg. He wrote saying he understood her indignation, but that he was satisfied with his performance under the circumstances and, furthermore, both Generals Pope and McClellan had praised his leadership in the battle. He enclosed these commendatory letters and added that she should be more circumspect in criticizing his superiors.

After General Grant had taken command of the Union Armies, Margaret voiced concern that George was not getting enough credit. But he had grown to appreciate Grant and was willing to work with him in a subordinate role, letting Grant take credit whenever it was offered. She continued to be very protective of George and, at one point, even suggested that he resign. There was little he could do about Margaret's concerns except to tell her that he doubted that the truth about his part in the war would ever be known or fully appreciated.

George took a Christmas leave in 1864, and they celebrated their first Christmas together in four years. Their festivities were dampened somewhat by the illness of their son John Sergeant. Although John was on his deathbed, Meade was needed at the front and left Margaret to cope with their son's illness alone. When their son eventually died, General Grant ordered a steamer to take George home.

When Lincoln was shot, Margaret draped the windows of their home in black and hung the old battle flags at half-mast. It was a sad day at the Meade home as it was in many homes.

George stayed in the Army after the war and was assigned to various commands that permitted him to use Philadelphia as a home base.

Margaret was taking a walk with George when he suddenly complained of severe pain. She got him home, but pneumonia coupled by his old war wounds proved fatal. He died in November 1872 at the age of 56 and was buried in Laurel Hill Cemetery in Philadelphia. His warhorse, Old Baldy, was brought out of retirement and, rider less, followed the procession to the grave. On the day of the funeral, all business was suspended and the city was draped in mourning.

After George's death, Margaret continued to work tirelessly for various charities, many of which she organized. Her favorite was raising $5,000 for the restoration of St. Philip's Episcopal Church in Atlanta, Georgia.

Major General George Meade led the Army of the Potomac during the last two years of the war and became a Union hero for his leadership at Gettysburg. Meade had considerable difficulty with the press and it was not kind to him, often ignoring him completely. He stayed in the Army after the war holding several command positions with his headquarters in his hometown, Philadelphia.

Arabella Griffith Barlow

"I Need to Get Through the Lines"

Arabella Barlow emerges as one of the true heroines of the Civil War. Nicknamed Belle, she was born Feb. 28, 1824 in Sommerville, New Jersey, the middle child between two boys. Her parents divorced when she was two, and her father was lost at sea the following year. Belle was sent to live with her maternal grandmother's cousin Eliza Wallace. This arrangement was to develop into a warm and caring relationship between the two that was to last almost 20 years. Belle was educated at St. Mary's Hall in Burlington, New Jersey until age 20 when she left to live in New York City. She served as a governess for the children of a prominent merchant's family and soon became a member of a group of middle class socialites and artists. She was regarded as brilliant and cultivated, an effective conversationalist who had read, thought and observed much.

How she came to meet Frances (Frank) Barlow, an ambitious Harvard educated New York lawyer is not clear, but one might presume they traveled in some of the same social circles.

They were married on April 20, 1861. Two days later, Frank left for a three-month tour of duty with the 12th New York Volunteers. He signed on as a private although his education afforded him a lieutenancy. He soon grew weary of enlisted life and eventually accepted an offer of a commission.

At 37, Belle was twelve years older than her husband and they often took some good-natured teasing about this age difference. For example, they visited a Mrs. Daly one afternoon and the maid informed her mistress that a young man and his mother were waiting in the parlor. Such slights did not seem to disturb the two, as they were both secure and comfortable in their relationship.

After his initial enlistment, Frank sought and was commissioned as a Lt. Colonel in the 61st New York Volunteers. Anticipating that they would be separated for long periods by the war and not wishing to sit home alone, Belle decided to join the U.S. Sanitary Commission as a nurse. This would allow her to be an active participant in the conflict as well as keeping her close to the Army of the Potomac and to Frank. Her seemingly inexhaustible energy and uncanny ability to quickly assess the needs of the wounded earned her the admiration of all.

In September 1862, Belle was in Baltimore when word came that a major battle was about to be fought near Sharpsburg, Maryland. The North referred to it as Antietam and it was to become the bloodiest single day encounter of the war. She hurried to the battlefield arriving in time to see Frank being brought in from the field in a "mortally wounded" condition. Undeterred, Belle dismissed the diagnosis and nursed him back to health. An official of the U.S. Sanitary Commission later recalled seeing Belle, serene and self-possessed, caring for her husband-colonel. For his valor and leadership at Antietam, Frank was promoted to brigadier general.

At Gettysburg, Belle continued her service as a nurse with the Army of the Potomac. After the first day of battle, a Confederate messenger came through the lines under a flag of truce with a message for Mrs. Barlow. Her husband had been seriously wounded, was being cared for by a Confederate doctor and had requested that his wife, a nurse in the Union Army, be informed of his condition.

When Belle's request for permission to go through the lines to help her husband was denied, she went to Culp's Hill, where the battle lines were very close together, and, at daybreak, made a dash into the Confederate lines. Protected by a flag of truce, she emerged from this bold and heroic act unscathed. The Confederates helped her find Frank and she nursed him back to health a second time. Convalescence from these wounds took six months. Frank later reminisced that she surely saved his life as doctors had diagnosed his wounds as too severe for him to survive. Belle modestly believed she was just doing her duty.

Regarding this event, Confederate General John Brown Gordon told one of the more notable human-interest tales of the Civil War. Gordon claimed that he was the Confederate officer who found Frank, gave him water, had him moved to the shade, and had a doctor examine his wounds. He was also responsible for sending word to Mrs. Barlow. The tale then shifts to a meeting of the two in post—war Washington where Gordon was a Senator and Barlow was serving in the House of Representatives. Each thought the other had been killed during the war. Delighted to be reacquainted; they went on to become life-long friends.

Harpers Weekly ran a profile on General Barlow that ended with the following tribute to Belle: "The men of General Barlow's division would never forgive his biographer who should omit to record the unwearied service in the hospitals and among the wounded and dying Union soldiers from the beginning of the war to this day, of (Barlow's) faithful and devoted wife."

Belle stayed close to Frank throughout the Richmond campaign and was working as a nurse near City Point, Virginia when she contracted a serious infection. She was taken back to Washington where she appeared to have made a recovery. However, upon returning to Virginia to see Frank, her illness reoccurred. Frank walked her to the hospital, she was returned to Washington where she died on July 27, 1864 without seeing him again. It is reported that she declined to send him notice of her condition. When he finally got word, he was engaged in the siege of Petersburg. He was granted a 15-day leave to attend to her funeral.

Dr. W. H. Reed, a Union physician, eulogized this remarkable woman with these words: "Arabella was neither conscious that she was working beyond her strength nor realized the extreme exhaustion of her system, so she fainted at her work . . . her sparkling wit, her brilliant intellect, her unfailing good humor, lighted up our moments of rest . . . her beautiful constancy and self sacrifice . . . the bright and genial companionship and glowing sympathies, her warmth and loving nature come back to me . . . make inadequate any tribute I could pay her . . ."

Harper's Weekly wrote on her passing on August 13, 1864: "Mrs. Barlow from the first has been among the most eminent of the many heroines in this war whose names are not mentioned loudly, but whose memory will be forever in the grateful hearts of their friends and country."

Her husband's deathbed wish to persuade the government to raise a monument commemorating her memory as well as those of many other women who provided loyal service to the Union cause proved futile.

Frank later married Ellen Shaw. She was the sister of the famed Colonel. Robert Shaw who commanded the all black 54th Massachusetts and led them into battle at Battery Wagner where he was killed.

Union Major General Frances C. Barlow was left for dead on the battlefield at Gettysburg but was nursed back to life. He was highly regarded for his fighting at Spotsylvania where his troops captured thirty stands of enemy colors and some 3,000 prisoners. After the Civil War, he returned to practicing law and was twice elected Secretary of State of New York as well as to the U. S. House of Representatives.

Jessie Benton Fremont

"Jessie was my best ally"

National Portrait Gallery
Smithsonian Institution

A powerful father on one side along with a formidable husband on the other, this remarkably strong minded woman, who was indeed "stronger that her sex," consistently found it difficult to restrict her behavior to the role expected of a mid-nineteenth century woman.

Born to caring parents and the privileged life, Jessie Ann Benton developed into an unusually determined and independent woman. Her father, Senator Thomas Benton of Tennessee, was a strong character who was also known for his integrity and the thoughtful and loving care with which he treated his family.

33

Her mother, Elizabeth McDonald Benton, was intellectually accomplished, gentile in manner and well read. Her position on slavery, a trait Jesse inherited, was unequivocal; when she inherited slaves from her father, she immediately set them free and continued to feed and support them until they could take care of themselves.

Jessie was born on May 31, 1824, the next to the eldest in the family that included two sisters and two brothers. The children were tutored in classical literature, Spanish, French along with basic academic subjects. When they traveled, the senator would bring along a valise with appropriate reading material to insure that any free time could be profitably spent.

As Jesse matured and started to show interest in young men, her family sent her to Miss English Female Seminary in the Georgetown section of Washington, DC. She was a restless student, who much preferred to be taught at home by tutors. She made no friends and resisted all efforts by the school staff encouraging her to conform. She frequently spoke out against popular social and political issues much to the dismay of her teachers and classmates. In near despair, she cut off her long hair and ran to her father pleading to be allowed to leave school. She had moved from being a tomboy to a rebel.

As the daughter of an influential U.S. Senator, Jesse was introduced to many of the leading personalities on the national scene. President Andrew Jackson, and future Presidents Franklin Pierce, James Buchanan, James Polk and Martin Van Buren. She was encouraged to actively participate in conversations with the many distinguished Benton dinner guests. This provided a rich opportunity for her to voice her opinions on social and political issues and defend them against her father's sophisticated associates, a rare opportunity for a young lady in pre-Civil War society.

While Jesse enjoyed all the privileges provided by her family's social lineage, John Charles Fremont was raised on the edges of Southern society. His mother, Anne Whiting Pryor, abandoned her husband to run off with John's father, Charles Fremont, a French émigré dance instructor living in Richmond, Virginia. John Charles was born in 1813 in Savannah Georgia. By his mid-twenties, he was employed by the U.S. Army Corps of Topographical Engineers doing wilderness surveys of the mid-western frontier.

John Fremont was described as a "lithe and handsome man whose piercing grey-blue eyes conveyed a Byronic intensity." Jesse was captivated and a two-year romance ensued. Her parents urged her to wait an additional year before getting married. Senator Benton sought to separate the two by using his influence to have John transferred to Iowa. Concurrently, Jesse was dispatched to Virginia to live with relatives. While there she became involved in a prank devised by her cousin Preston Johnson, a West Point cadet. Since most family members thought the two looked alike, Preston suggested they change clothes and see how far they could carry out the deception. Confusion reigned briefly until they were discovered and the two fled with great mirth leaving the other guest bewildered and upset at this most unexpected behavior on the part of a southern belle. In her later years, Jesse enjoyed telling this story.

All these parental impediments proved in vain, as the couple eloped in October 1841. John was twenty-eight, Jesse seventeen. The elopement was planned to take advantage of Senator Benson absence from Washington. Once notified, his reaction was predictably one of outrage. This resulted in the newlyweds being banned from the family home. Jessie's mother pleaded with her husband seeking a reconciliation which, over a period of time, eventually took place and the outcasts where permitted to return.

John Fremont returned to his work exploring the Western United States culminating in the charting of the Oregon Tail. Jesse was left alone to wait often encumbered by pregnancies and the burden of caring for small children. She was ultimately to bear five children, two of whom died in infancy. During this time Jesse was to discover what she called her "most happy life work." When John returned from one expedition and was faced with the task of writing up the required governmental report, Jesse eagerly volunteered her services. This was the start of lifetime collaboration between husband and wife that benefited both. Together they produced vivid and readably reports that became best sellers. Published by the Congress to great acclaim, they solidified John's stature as a great explorer and national hero. Later, Jesse was to characterize her role in this joint venture as "secretary and other self," a depiction that elevated her work from being merely clerical to that of a full partnership.

In 1849, while John trekked to California overland, Jessie and her two children started on the route through Panama. Early on this trip her son became ill and died. Jesse was inconsolable but finally had the body sent home with friends and continued the trip and their six-year old daughter. They crossed the Isthmus of Panama in a dugout canoe and mule back to join him. She described this experience as a "living nightmare." When she got to the Pacific coast there were no ships waiting for the follow on trip to San Francisco. She waited amid the rain and mosquitoes becoming quite ill and coughing up blood. All in all, the journey was a painful tribute to her fortitude and determination. This was to be the first, and most trying, of the four trips she was eventually to make to California culminating in 1878 when she was able to travel in relative comfort by train.

Shortly after her reunion with John, his Las Mariposa mine struck gold. The Fremonts were now very rich and, consequently, their lives underwent a dramatic change. Unaccustomed to managing a household by herself, she experienced some difficulties. When a Texan suggested that she purchase one of his slaves to help, Jessie declined and thus endeared herself to the anti-slavery groups in California.

In 1850, John was elected to the U. S. Senate. Jesse thoroughly enjoyed being a senator's wife. She relished all the social amenities associated with the office, which included an opportunity to socialize with the Washington elite such as Daniel Webster and Henry Wadsworth Longfellow. She had many interesting stories to tell and a capacity to tell them well which made her a great favorite.

At age thirty-three in 1855, Jesse gave birth to their last child, a boy named Frances Preston. In 1856, capitalizing on his fame as a celebrated explorer, he was nominated by the newly formed Republican Party as its presidential candidate on an anti-slavery platform.

From the pages of the New York Tribune, Horace Greeley predicted certain victory for Fremont. The campaign provided Jesse with opportunity to excel as political advisor, speechwriter and all round helpmate. In what became labeled the "Fremont and Jessie" campaign, she was a whirlwind of activity, managing correspondence, attending to public relations and writing a campaign biography. Although she was careful to remain discreet, she became a crowd favorite as spontaneous shouts of "Jessie, Jessie, Give us Jessie" forced her to make repeated platform appearances.

Jessie's father did not support Fremont's candidacy campaigning for his opponent instead causing considerable tension within the family. Fremont's loss to James Buchanan was a severe letdown for Jesse. Rumors of John's infidelity, kept quite during the presidential race, reemerged causing Jesse to become deeply depressed.

When John returned to California to supervise his mining interest, Jesse took the children to Europe for an extended stay. Separation brought reflection, however, for she wrote from Paris that she loved him more then than ever before. The frequent pattern of withdrawal and reunion that was repeatedly to characterize their union manifested itself once again.

With the outbreak of war, President Lincoln offered Fremont Command of the Western Department, which he accepted. Jessie plunged into her new role as supportive wife with all the vigor natural to her personality. She was in her element sharing his problems and offering solutions. She soon got involved in helping solve the many problems associated with John's command from buying arms to procuring money and recruiting staff. Rumors surfaced about "General Jessie," but she was so occupied being "secretary and other self" to her beleaguered husband to pay much attention.

In spite of Jesse's enthusiastic support and assistance, John Fremont was unable to bring to war fighting the same success he had demonstrated as an explorer. When he declared martial law in Missouri and unilaterally decided to free the slaves, President Lincoln relieved him of command.

Jessie was furious at Lincoln's decision and decided to go to Washington to plead her husbands cause. After spending two days in dirty, smoky, railroad cars, she arrived in the capitol and went directly to the President's office taking Judge Edward Coles, the abolitionist leader, with her. After listening impatiently to Jessie outline her husband's case, the President sternly told her that the war was not about the Negro, it was about saving the Union. Lincoln, who told Jesse she was "quite a female politician," was thoroughly exasperated by her, claiming that he had to "exercise all the awkward tact I have to avoid quarrelling with her." When Jessie learned of the President's reaction to her visit, she noted that when a man expresses himself with conviction, he is considered forceful but when a woman speaks out earnestly, "she is reported as a lady who has lost her temper."

Following the war, the Fremonts used their gold rush fortune to purchase an elegant estate on the Hudson River in New York. Jessie spent the next 10 years here raising her children and enjoying a well-earned spell of luxurious domesticity. She also made peace with her father who was a frequent visitor.

In the summer of 1869, the Fremonts embarked on the *Ville de Paris* for the voyage to the French capitol. Here, ensconced in opulent quarters next to the Tuileries, Jesse and her daughter Lily, embarked on grand shopping expeditions returning laden with trunks and bonnet boxes. The two visited Germany and Denmark and later, the Austrian Alps. John was only occasionally with them having developed a romantic relationship with the beautiful young sculptress Vinnie Ream. The two saw each other daily and also corresponded with what John called "love letters." Jessie later posed for Miss Ream for a bust commissioned by her husband.

John and Jessie returned in late fall to face financial difficulties that became increasingly troublesome over the next few years. In 1873, John was tried and convicted in French court of a $6,000,000 swindling charge. He received a five-year sentence in absentia. That September, the Fremonts suffered another financial blow when a large Wall Street banking firm collapsed plunging the nation into financial crisis. The family fortune had evaporated almost overnight. They were forced to sell the house on the Hudson and suffer the humiliation of putting their furniture, books, and paintings up for auction. The opulent lifestyle they had long enjoyed was gone and they were now faced with adjusting to living in genteel poverty.

Motivated by financial need, Jessie turned to writing professionally. Her efforts included everything from personal reminiscences to children's stories. Her efforts were greeted with mixed results financially. Encouraged by the great success, which greeted General Grant's memoirs, she wrote John's life story but the market for the biography of a discredited old soldier was not strong. She was, however, able to keep the family a float during this dry spell.

Further relief came in 1878, when President Hayes, who supported John when he ran for the presidency, appointed John as the territorial governor of the

Arizona Territory. They journeyed to this new post by way of California where they were received with great enthusiasm. An exhausted Jesse was revived by the reception. One lawyer exclaimed that he came to see John Fremont, but to "honor Jessie." The legendary "Pathfinder" still generated interest but it was the vibrant, courageous, and ever faithful Jesse who commanded their respect and admiration. The aging Fremont needed her more than ever and she responded by supporting him and defending his tarnished honor to the very end.

Even more financial relief came when in March 1890, Congress passed a pension bill authorizing him a major general's retirement income of $6,000 a year for life. When he died, Jessie was also voted an annual pension of $2,000.

Unexpectedly, in July 1890, the 77-year old John Fremont died of peritonitis. Jessie's 12 years of widowhood where spent in California until her death in 1902 at age 78. A portrait of John in his full Civil War uniform hung over her desk. She wrote that it was a "true shrine, we keep flowers there always."

Her ashes were placed beside John at the Rockland Cemetery on the Hudson.

Major General John C. Fremont an experienced explorer of the west and a major general during the Civil War. Before the war he made a vast fortune from gold in California. In his later life he lost this wealth and served for nine years as governor of the Arizona Territory. He died in 1890 and was buried in Rockland Cemetery in New York.

Fanny Adams Chamberlain

The Sophisticated Lady

Courtesy of Pejepscot Historical Society

"There are many, many things that I would say to you, my dearest Lawrence . . . but I cannot write *freely* because I am afraid that what I may say will not be sacred to you alone."

This letter written in late February 1854 when the future Mrs. Chamberlain was teaching in Milledgeville, Georgia does much to explain why there is such a paucity of first-hand personal information on this enigmatic lady. She understood Chamberlain's propensity to share her letters with members of his family and hence was reluctant to express her emotions too openly.

Fanny, born Caroline Frances Adams in 1825, was the seventh and last child of Ashur Adams and his third wife, Amelia Wyllis Adams. Distant cousins of the John Adams family and descendants of Mayflower colonist, Miles Standish, the family was poor but proud of their heritage. Her father, aging and enfeebled with illness, could not cope with their youngest daughter's needs. At age four, she was sent to live with her childless cousin, the Reverend George Adams and his wife, Sarah Ann of Brunswick, Maine, as their daughter. Fanny was henceforth always to call her new adoptive parents, father and mother. The Adams grew to be delighted with their new charge. Mrs. Adams, a kindly lady given to simple dress appropriate to a minister's wife, indulged her suppressed taste for finery by dressing the little girl. One photograph captures little Fanny in a beautiful scarlet dress trimmed in black velvet with a charming hat to match. This was to foretell the fascination and appreciation the grown-up Fanny was to have for beautiful and fancy clothing.

Until she was twelve years old, contact and correspondence with her birth family was limited. By 1840 however, she seemed to have developed an affectionate relationship with her mother. Emily, a deeply religious person, reassured Fanny of her Boston family's love for her and reminded her of the obligation she had toward her adoptive parents.

At 18, as Fanny was finishing her education at Brunswick's high school, she wrote a paper that testifies to her lively sense of humor. Asked to compose a theme using verbs ending in "fy", she worked in a subtle apology for causing mischief in class: "This is to certify, notify, exemplify, testify, and signify my obedient disposition; and I hope that it will gratify, satisfy, beautify and edify my teacher, and pacify, modify, mollify and nullify his feelings of dissatisfaction towards me . . . Please do not exclaim 'O fie!' when reading this paper."

Fanny's adopted family held artistic accomplishment in high regard. The Rev. Adams recorded this in his diary in 1842: "The world of art must be the highest, the most ideal, wherein every pang dissolves into a greater pleasure, and where we resemble men on mountain tops; the storm which burst heavily on the real life of the world below is to us but a cooling shower." Fanny would quickly move beyond the superficial in the world of the arts. She studied painting with Maine's premier portrait artist, Jeremiah Hardy, and music from the Portland organist, Henry S. Edwards, considered to be the best teacher in the state.

Prior to coming to Brunswick, Reverend Adams had taught classical literature at the Bangor Theological Seminary and was a voracious reader of the great poets, dramatists and novelists. This interest was transferred to his adopted daughter and by age 15, Fanny was fully participating in Brunswick's literary discussion groups. The precocious teenager took this role seriously and was not reluctant to offer her well-reasoned opinions on discussion topics and theories. The rich intellectual atmosphere of her Brunswick home encouraged her to express herself. Such liberties were not always considered appropriate to well-bred young women of her time. Fanny's willingness to display her intellectual repertoire "startled some and intrigued others."

Although she continued to attend her father's church and played the organ for the choir, she stubbornly refused to accept the dogma of Congregationalism. Even as she strove to be the obedient daughter in all things, the continued disagreements over her religious beliefs were a source of painful discomfort to Reverend Adams.

By age 26, she was becoming increasingly aware of the tall, serious Bowdoin student who had become director of her father's choir. Together Lawrence Chamberlain and Fanny faithfully attended Harriet Beecher Stowe readings of Uncle Tom's Cabin, the book that would make the author's name renown throughout the world. "Fanny and Lawrence found much to admire in one another," writes biographer Diane Smith, "but this would be no mere meeting of minds. Admiration became powerful attractions, and attractions turned to love during an intense and rather tumultuous courtship."

What are we to make of the young suitor's chances? Initially, he had much to overcome. First, Fanny was two years older. This head start gave her a degree of sophistication in the arts, music, and society in general that left Lawrence feeling like the country bumpkin in her presence. She was the daughter of a prominent clergyman and moved freely through the upper levels of Portland and Brunswick society thereby exposing her to elite elements of both worlds. And finally, Reverend Adams did not initially feel Lawrence was a suitable match for his intellectual daughter.

But Lawrence was determined to woo her and win her and by mid May 1852, Fanny had declared her love and agreed to marry him. However, the courtship was protracted and distant when Fanny accepted a teaching position in Georgia and the two lovers were separated for the better part of the next three years. Their letters during this time bear testimony to the evolution of their relationship and included teasing comments that sought to elicit total commitment and reassurances that this was a "first love" for them both. Lawrence was by far the most prolific in these exchanges as Fanny continued to express fears that he was sharing her correspondence with others. In February she wrote, " . . . I would give the world to feel that every word between us was sacred to us alone; then I could tell you every thought and feeling in my letters, just as freely as I would whisper them into your ear, if I were resting in your bosom as of old."

Finally, the long and distant courtship ended and Lawrence and Fanny were wed on December 7, 1855, in a ceremony performed by her adopted father.

After marriage, the self-reliant 30-year-old bride and the newly installed Brunswick college instructor seemed to have achieved a comfortable balance in their relationship. Although, Lawrence, in keeping with the prevailing nineteenth century patriarchal views, referred to Fanny as his "little wife", he was also careful to consider her opinions in making decisions that affected their lives together. A letter written after their marriage, reflecting back on their wedding night, brought forth the following uncharacteristically romantic recollection from Fanny as she shared her memories of the "*dear* little sacred chamber where I first pillowed my head upon your bosom—your own beloved wife."

Ten months later in October 1856, their daughter, Grace Dupree, nicknamed Daisy was born. Following a premature baby that died the next year, a healthy boy named Harold Wyllis arrived in the fall of 1858, but this was followed by the loss of two more daughters who did not survive their first year. Despite these painful loses and the financial difficulties experienced during these years, the Chamberlains were thankful for their two healthy children, their new home, and good prospects for the future when, like so many other families of the era, the Civil War intervened.

In August 1862, Lawrence accepted Maine governor Israel Washburn's offer of a commission as a Lt. Colonel of the 20th Maine volunteers. His unilateral decision to join the Army was to be the first serious breach in their union and severely altered their relationship. He came to fully embrace being a soldier and became eager to see battle, telling Fanny that he could not imagine ever being a college professor again. After facing the dangers and hardships of the battle for Little Round Top at Gettysburg, he wrote to Fanny, "We are fighting gloriously. Our loss is terrible, but we are beating the Rebels as they have never been beaten before. The 20th has immortalized itself." One can imagine her reaction to such an enthusiastic outburst on his part toward a war that had cost her so dearly by separating her from her husband and the children from their father.

In June 1864, her loss almost became permanent when Chamberlain was severely wounded during the battle for Petersburg. On what he thought was his deathbed, Lawrence wrote, "To know and love you makes life and death beautiful" and to "Cherish the darlings." To everyone's amazement, he survived and Fanny rushed to Annapolis to be at his side and nurse him during his convalescence. Against his wife's persistent wishes, his dedication to the Union prevailed and he returned to soldering till the very end. His heroics during the war earned him the gratitude of General Grant who honored Lawrence by appointing him as the Union officer designated to accept the final surrender of the Confederate Army at Appomattox.

The war's end left the Chamberlains in an emotional abyss. The process of adjusting to civilian life created great emotional stress for them both. Lawrence briefly returned to teaching at Bowdoin but quickly found academic life to be unsatisfactory after the excitement of the war years. In 1866 he accepted the Maine Republican Party's nomination as a gubernatorial candidate. Elected, he went on to serve four one-year terms. This new career in politics led to great dissatisfaction in Fanny's life. She became moody and depressed, finding it difficult to adjust to her husband's political friends and the fact that he was constantly away from their home in Brunswick either on the Civil War lecture tour or in Augusta on state government business. At one point in 1868, as a reaction to the increasing estrangement, a separation was discussed. This radical development came about when Lawrence learned that Fanny was telling neighbors that he was pulling her hair and abusing her in other ways, and she was seeking a divorce. He endured a restless night before responding and when he did he chose his words wisely. Ignoring the accusations, he wrote that he would not deny her a divorce if that was her wish but added, "I should think we had skill enough to adjust the terms of a separation without the wretchedness to all our family."

This calm, rational approach seems to have cooled Fanny's emotions and over time, the Chamberlains were able to work out their marital difficulties. In 1878, the entire family, including 21-year-old Grace and 19-year-old Wyllis enjoyed a memorable European holiday that brought them all closer together. Later, as Lawrence's various business ventures drew them apart, his letters to Fanny displayed some of the tenderness of earlier times. In 1890 he wrote," I have your beautiful letter that quickens all my great love for you so that I am impatient of any condition that seems to keep you away from me."

By the late 1880s, Fanny and Lawrence were both suffering from various physical ills: his war wounds had never healed properly thereby causing great pain, and her eyesight continued to worsen until she lost her sight completely. In the summer of 1905, Fanny fell and broke her hip. By October, shortly after her 80th birthday, she died and was buried in Brunswick's Pine Grove Cemetery. The back of her tombstone bears the mysterious engraving "Unveiled." Lawrence survived her by nine years.

The war that had torn the nation apart had also divided this couple as well. It is a tribute to their character that Fanny and Lawrence were able to recognize the value of their marriage and rekindle the old tenderness they had once shared for each other.

Major General Joshua Lawrence Chamberlain earned the Congressional Medal of Honor for his heroic defense of Little Round Top at Gettysburg. His postwar accomplishments include being elected four-term governor of Maine as well as president of Bowdoin College in Brunswick Maine.

Mary Ann Montgomery Forrest

"Like a True Soldier"

Mary Ann by Paul Strain copyright 2005

In April 1845, Mary Ann Montgomery and her mother were on their way to church when their wagon became stuck in a muddy streambed. As the two ladies were becoming increasingly concerned with their plight, a horseman came by, saw their predicament, waded into the muddy morass, and rescued them. He then helped the driver push the carriage to dry ground. While this was going on, he also noticed two young men standing around who had made no effort to help the ladies. Irritated with their conduct, he ordered them to move on or face a certain thrashing at his hand. Then, Nathan Bedford Forrest introduced himself to Mary Ann and her mother. They were impressed. Taking advantage of the moment, he asked if he could visit Mary Ann, and her mother readily agreed.

Mary Ann Montgomery was the daughter of Presbyterian minister William H. and Elizabeth Cowen Montgomery. The family tree on William's side went back to General Richard Montgomery of Revolutionary War fame that was killed in the attack on Quebec. When Mary Ann's father died, Elizabeth's brother, Samuel Cowan, became the family guardian. He was also a Presbyterian minister. Mary Ann was described as having refined taste, being religiously inclined, and having been brought up with strong family ties.

On their third visit, Nathan asked Mary Ann for her hand in marriage; she accepted and her mother concurred. But, her uncle, the Reverend Cowan did not. He told the aspirant that his disapproval was based on Nathan's character defects, which included cussing and gambling. Mary Ann, being a good Christian girl, needed a more suitable husband. Nathan, replied, "I know it and that's why I want her." Her uncle relented and married them in September 1845.

Mary Ann and Nathan lived first in Mississippi but soon moved to Memphis where Nathan became very successful as a real estate investor, politician, and a slave trader. Colonel George Adair, a close friend of the Forrests, offered these comments in describing Nathan's *modus operandi* as a slaver, "He was always careful when he purchased a married slave to use every effort to secure also the husband or the wife, as the case might be, and unite them, and in handling children he would not permit the separation of a family."

There was good money in the slave trade and, along with his other holdings; Forrest was reportedly worth $1,500,000 at the time of the Civil War.

In 1846, William Montgomery Forrest was born followed two years later by Fanny who died at age five. Mary Ann was devoted to her family while Nathan was described as firm yet sympathetic. They had been married 16 years when war occurred and, over that time, they had developed a loving and carrying relationship that was to serve them well during the coming crisis.

Nathan raised and funded his own mounted battalion and led it off to war as its commander. Uneducated though not illiterate and completely unschooled in military affairs, he quickly developed into a resourceful and natural cavalry tactician as several Union commanders from Grant to Sherman and Sheridan were soon to learn.

When William, their 15-year-old son, went to war as an aide to his father, Mary Ann had two reasons to stay as close to the battlefield as possible, often traveling in a specially designated ambulance. With both a husband and a son in constant danger, the war years represented a continuous source of anguish for Mary Ann but, as is often the way with women during wartime, she made no complaints that have been recorded. She seemed to accept the military risks and dangers facing her men but she did worry about the lack of suitable peer companionship for her son. To address his wife's concern, Forrest sought to "borrow" two companions for Willie, the sons of an Episcopal bishop and a

Confederate general. On the first night of the battle of Shiloh, the youngsters were missing. They eventually turned up safe proudly displaying a dozen Federal prisoners they had captured.

In 1865 the Memphis *Avalanche-Appeal* offered a portrait of Mary Ann's character during the war, " . . . apparently delicate, but with great reserve force and powers of endurance . . ." She, "survived the privations, inconveniences and exposures of four years, moving from place to place as the scenes of war shifted, like a true soldier."

The Forrests lost much of their fortune during the war and a sustained effort was required to rebuild their real estate holdings. Nathan was proud of Mary Ann's efforts at domestication, such as making butter and raising chickens.

Realizing that they were still better off than most of their antebellum countrymen, they voluntarily provided aid to Confederate veterans and their families. Nathan also assisted several ex-Union officers by renting them land for development purposes.

Throughout their years together, Mary Ann never abandoned her efforts to get Nathan to accept the Christian faith. Finally, in 1875, with her on his arm, he walked into the Presbyterian Church and told the minister he was ready to become a Christian. Mary Ann's persistent and gentle ways had won him over. Gaining her life's most sought ambition was a great relief to her in their declining years.

In 1877 Nathan became very ill, probably from diabetes. Mary Ann took him to Hurricane Springs, Georgia in hopes of providing some relief, but this did little to help his deteriorating condition. She tried to help him by managing his diet to which Nathan retorted, "I know Mary is the best friend I have on earth, but sometimes it does seem that she is determined to starve me to death." He did recognize the loving influence she exerted on his behalf and later mentioned that he was sure that Mary Ann's prayers throughout the years had spared his life.

Later that year Nathan died at age of 55. Jefferson Davis delivered the funeral oration. When her son William's wife died young, Mary Ann raised her three grandchildren. She also continued Nathan's commitment to provide aid to the wives and children of Confederate veterans. Mary Ann survived her husband by 15 years. She died from heart failure in 1892. They are buried together under the Forrest Equestrian Statue in Forrest Park in Memphis.

Lieutenant General Nathan Bedford Forrest was an effective cavalry commander and a constant menace to Union armies in the west. His war record and associated stories have become legendary. After the war he urged a peaceful return to the union and he and his wife contributed to aiding the families of Civil War veterans, both South and North.

Julia Dent Grant

"General Grant was the very nicest and handsomest man I ever saw"

Picture History

Frederick Dent, a southerner by birth and inclination, was a successful St. Louis planter who had 18 slaves to work his 1,000-acre White Haven Plantation. Like many of his planter contemporaries, Dent acquired the title of Colonel, an honorary title of respect and esteem. He and his wife Ellen raised eight children and were able to provide a solid upbringing for them all. Ellen had been well educated and wanted to be sure that her children received the same advantage, including the girls.

Julia Boggs Dent, the first daughter, was born on January 26, 1826. In the family hierarchy, she was situated between four older brothers, whom she idolized, and three younger sisters. Julia has been described as a plain-looking, stocky youngster with a noticeable eye deformity. But she more than made up for these physical limitations by an abundance of charm and a fine sense of humor.

Her idyllic life at White Haven came to an abrupt halt at age 10 when she experienced academic difficulties and was sent off to Mauro Boarding School in St. Louis. She eventual overcame the loneliness of being separated from her family as her strength of character and overall friendliness came to prevail. She remembered the years there as being occupied in reading romantic novels and having great difficulties with Roman numerals. It was here that she read *The Dashing Lieutenant,* a book that gave her vital insights into a life style of an Army wife.

After seven years, Julia returned home eager to apply her recently acquired social skills. Young officers stationed nearby at Jefferson Barracks were often invited to social functions at the Dent house. Since Ulysses had been the roommate of Julia's brother Frederick Dent, he was often among the invited. Another favorite was Lt. James Longstreet who was destined to become General Robert E. Lee's "War Horse" during the War. Longstreet, who was also Julia's cousin, later referred to these visits and remembered Grant as "the man who was to eclipse us all . . . of noble, generous heart, a lovable character, a valued friend."

Ulysses was almost immediately attracted to Julia. As Longstreet recalled, "We visited the Dent home for his (Ulysses) first visit with Julia—a charming woman who five years later would become Mrs. Grant. She was a frequent visitor to the garrison balls and hops . . . (and) was something of a tease." Although she lacked classic beauty she was lively and personable. Only five feet tall, she appeared to be fragile but was an avid horsewoman and very comfortable in an outdoor environment.

Ulysses' interest in Julia continued and he eventually asked her to wear his West Point ring, an offer she declined. When she received word that her suitor might be preparing to ship out, she quickly reconsidered her earlier decision and rode out to the Army camp only to find that Ulysses was indeed gone. A fellow officer quickly notified Grant that Julia was asking for him. Grant's regiment was enroute to Louisiana when this news reached him. He had to be satisfied that he had at least an informal engagement as yet unblessed by parental approval.

Colonel Dent had serious apprehensions about his favorite daughter being happy as an officer's wife. At one point he even suggested that Ulysses marry Nellie, Julia's younger sister. Eventually it was Ellen Dent who saw promise in the young Ulysses even though she had doubts about Julia's suitability as an Army wife.

The Mexican War kept Ulysses a long way from St. Louis for about two years. The young couple's separation was bridged somewhat by letter writing, which attested to a strong bond that had developed between the two. Julia anticipated his return eagerly and needed no urging to pursue a wedding date. Overcoming parental concerns, she and Ulysses was married on August 22, 1848, at the Dent homestead. None of the Grant family attended the ceremony. Ulysses took Julia to Bethel, Ohio to meet his family. It was to be the first time she had left St. Louis and her first boat trip.

Ulysses had been assigned to Detroit and he assumed Julia would soon follow. But she missed her family so badly that the mere thought of leaving home brought her to tears. Her father proposed that she stay at home and that Ulysses could visit her a few times each year when he could get leave. Ulysses left the decision to Julia, and she ultimately decided to join him.

In Detroit, they attended parties, took lake cruises and generally enjoyed newlywed life, which included Julia's attempts at learning how to cook and maintain a household. By 1850, Julia was pregnant and, on the advice of the regimental doctor, returned home to St. Louis to have the baby. A son to be christened Frederick was born on May 30 and Ulysses took leave to be with her. A second son, named Ulysses was born in 1852 while Julia was staying with Grant's parents in Ohio. Because of his birthplace, he was called "Buckeye," later shortened to Buck. They had two additional children, Ellen (Nellie) born in 1855 and Jesse Root born in 1858.

On July 5, 1852 Grant sailed to his new assignment on the west coast without his family. Julia missed him dearly for the next two years but he remained largely unaware of her deeper feelings since she was such a notoriously lax letter writer. His letters consistently described how lonely he was without her, which finally led to his decision to leave the Army.

He returned to St. Louis and built a log cabin on land provided by Julia's father. They called the farm "Hardscrabble". Julia was forced to face the task of trying to run a household without servants. She had difficulties with cooking and managing domestic accounts and did not enjoy living in a log cabin, which compared so unfavorably to her childhood home. The Panic of 1857 brought financial ruin to Grant's farming plans and by 1860, the Grants were living in Galena, Illinois where he was employed in his father's tanning business.

When the war broke out, Col. Dent supported the Confederacy and broke off all contact with Grant. With the passage of time, however, as Ulysses' fame achieved national prominence, this attitude changed and he was to grow proud of his son-in-law's accomplishments.

The Grants were very fortunate among Civil War families in that Julia was able to accompany him to many of his postings. As he advanced in rank and prominence, this became easier and Julia went everywhere, short of actual battlefield conditions. She brought a welcomed domesticity to his camps as well as nursing him through his frequent migraine headaches.

At Holly Springs, she just barely avoided the arrival of rebel forces to make her escape. When Ulysses fell from his horse and was bedridden in New Orleans, she arrived to nurse him. She viewed him as her husband/hero and would do all she could to make his life as pleasant as possible under trying conditions. When Ulysses was appointed Commander of the Union Armies, President Abraham Lincoln encouraged her presence, confidant that his senior Army commander was at his best when she was nearby,

In February 1865, Union Major General Edward Ord and Confederate Major General Longstreet met to discuss prisoner exchange. During this meeting General Ord offered a proposal to end the war by way of a negotiated peace settlement between Generals Lee and Grant. Since Julia Grant and Louise Longstreet were friends, it was suggested that they could help bring the two sides to the bargaining table. On his side, Longstreet discussed the idea with Jefferson Davis and Lee. This appears to have been taken seriously enough for a dispatch to be sent to Lynchburg requesting that Louise come to Richmond. On March 3rd Grant received word from Lee inquiring if there was "the possibility of arriving at a satisfactory adjustment of the present unhappy difficulties by means of a military convention." He added that he was authorized to do whatever such a convention might advise. For her part, Julia was thrilled and enchanted with the idea of taking part in such a noble venture and pleaded with her husband to be allowed to participate. But Grant was adamant declaring: "It is simply absurd. The men have fought this war and the men will finish it." He then informed Lee that he was not authorized to discuss peace terms in the field and that such powers rested in the hands of the President alone, a clear sign that the President was holding out for total and unconditional surrender.

Towards war's end, and at Julia's suggestion, the President and Mrs. Lincoln decided to visit Grant's headquarters at City Point, Virginia. It was during this visit by the first couple that Julia was first exposed to Mary Lincoln's often irrational and spiteful behavior. One particular episode involved Mary Ord, wife of General Ord, then commander of the Army of the James. When the President's wife learned that Mary Ord had been out horseback riding by the side of the President, she became irate since she "never allowed the President to see any woman alone." When Julia attempted to mollify her she heatedly replied, "I suppose you think you'll get to the White House yourself, don't you?" Julia was learning to be leery of Mary Lincoln.

After the fall of Richmond, Julia visited the former Confederate capital, greatly distressed at the terrible human cost of war. Upon her return she learned that the Lincolns had failed to invite her to a going away party on their boat. She promptly embarked on a James River cruise boat with her friends. As her boat passed the presidential vessel she ordered the band to play "Now You'll Remember Me." a childish but satisfying act of retribution.

A long overdue visit to the children served as a legitimate excuse for Julia's decision on April 13th to turn down the Lincolns theater invitation for the following evening. The Grants were already in Philadelphia when news arrived of John Wilkes Booth's infamous act. Grant later regretted being absence that fateful evening, thinking he might have acted to prevent the assassination.

The war's end, the assassination, and the turmoil that followed catapulted the Grants into the national spotlight. The unsuccessful farmer was now the gracious recipient of gifts and honoraria that included houses in Galena, Ohio; Philadelphia; and New York. Fame and prosperity were at hand and by 1868, he was worth $750,000 and was able to give Julia an allowance of $1,000 a month. They had come a long way from the desolation, grit, and stench of his father's tannery.

Julia Grant served for a full eight years as first lady, the first to do so since Elizabeth Monroe. People loved her style, in contrast to the staid and stuffy Mrs. Lincoln. She invited her father to move into the White House so he could be looked after. She thoroughly enjoyed being the President's wife and worked diligently to make the social activities attendant to the Grant administration enjoyable. Toward that end, she was fortunate to have the help of Julia Fish, wife of the Secretary of State, a socially experienced and prominent Washington socialite. She helped Mrs. Grant make her way thru the many pitfalls of White House social life with ease. On Tuesdays she held receptions for all interested citizens. When asked if "colored" folks should be included, Julia replied, "Admit them all." However, behind her back, her instructions were often ignored. Regardless of her enthusiasm for the role, she had only a modicum of influence on her husband's administration. Her primary responsibility was to oversee a smoothly functioning White House, catering to the cultural and social needs of the presidency. Her last act was to arrange a luncheon for the incoming Hayes administration on Inauguration Day. Her attachment to the White House was so deep that tears marked her final farewell.

Her energies now turned to making the necessary plans for a two and a half year world tour. Julia and Ulysses had a grand time. This odyssey, that included an audience with Queen Victoria as well as dining with the mandarins of the Chinese court offered once in a lifetime social opportunities that especially appealed to Julia's love of pomp and ceremony. They returned from Europe in 1879.

When Grant failed to win the Republican nomination at the 1880 convention, the Grants moved to New York where Ulysses became a silent partner in the firm of Grant and Ward. When this venture collapsed in 1884, they faced financial ruin. Since Grant had resigned his commission at war's end instead of retiring, it bared him from receiving a pension. His good friend William Sherman, aware that Grant was dying and anticipating the financial difficulties facing Julia upon his death, took up his cause in Washington. Through his lobbying efforts and the cooperation of several key congressmen, a pension bill was passed that awarded Ulysses $13,500 a year and Julia $5,000. Upon being notified Grant simply said, "I am grateful the thing has passed." Julia was overjoyed, "Hurrah, our old commander is back."

Diagnosed with incurable throat cancer, Grant spent the last years of his life writing his war memoirs hoping to provide enough income to sustain Julia after his death. Mark Twain provided vital support to this eleventh hour literary effort and saw it through to publication. Shortly after Ulysses' death in 1885, Twain was able to present Julia with a royalty check for $200,000. The book went on to be extremely successful and would eventually generate over $450,000 in income permitting Julia to live a very comfortable life.

She continued to live in New York City, worked for women's suffrage and enjoyed her grandchildren. She was the first president's wife to write her memoirs, which were not published until 1975. Such an inordinate delay can be partially explained by a granddaughter who recalled her saying, "I don't want all this published for several generations. Some one might get mad, because I'm telling how they really felt and acted."

Eventually, Julia became good friends with Varina Davis, wife of the former Confederate President Jefferson Davis. Looking back on her life, Julia was quoted as saying; "One must not deem me partial if I say General Grant was the very nicest and handsomest man I ever saw . . ." She later wrote, summarizing their years together, " . . . the light of his glorious fame still reaches out to me, falls upon me, and warms me."

Julia died in Washington D. C. in 1904, outliving Ulysses by 17 years, and is entombed beside him at Riverside Park in New York City.

General Grant first came to national attention for distinguished service in Mexico. With the capture of Forts Henry and Donelson followed by his success at Vicksburg in July 1863, he became General-in-Chief of all Union Forces and served in this capacity to the end of the war. He later was elected president of the U.S. for two terms.

Susan Tarleton

"It was a wonderful courtship, but . . ."

War is often tragically disruptive to affairs of the heart. The sad experience of Susan Tarleton is very similar to what also happened to Catherine Hewitt when her fiancée, Union General John Reynolds was killed on the first day of the Battle of Gettysburg. Susan was to suffer a similar fate several months later.

Susan was honored to be the maid of honor at the wedding of General William J. Hardee and Miss Mary Lewis in January 1864. This event introduced her to the best man; the 36-year old bachelor general, Patrick Ronayne Cleburne and she was much impressed. For his part, the dashing Confederate hero was very much taken by the 24-year-old beauty and quickly decided that he wanted to marry her. Wartime seems to hasten romance.

Following the Hardee wedding, as was customary, the entire wedding party set out on a several day steamboat trip to Mobile. The journey turned into a leisurely and romantic time of courtship for the newly acquainted couple and they soon found they very much enjoyed each other's company. Susan proved to be not only very attractive but also charming, witty, and vivacious. Cleburne stayed on in Mobile for several days and continued to press his cause. Although shy and a bit overwhelmed by the attention of this famous general, she offered little resistance to his continued advances.

Susan was the eldest daughter of George W. Tarleton a successful Mobile businessman. They lived in a fine brick house on the corner of St. Louis and Claiborne Streets. (Speculation has it that Cleburne told Susan he would see to changing the spelling of Claiborne Street once they were married.) Although Susan's father was a native of New Hampshire and a Yankee sympathizer, all his children were dedicated to the southern cause.

Patrick was born in Ireland. His father was a physician and Patrick was raised with the comforts of middle class society. His mother died when he was 18 months old followed by his father's death when he was 15. He came to America in 1849, became a naturalized citizen in 1856, and started a successful law practice. He joined the Confederate army as a captain and quickly rose to the rank of general becoming the only Irish born soldier to achieve this grade.

Susan and Patrick went on long walks, sang songs while she played the piano, and attended church together. Susan was saddened by news that her suitor was soon to be called back to duty but prior to leaving, he proposed. Although flattered by this precipitous declaration, she still held back while promising to write.

Patrick returned to his unit in high spirits and hoped he would be allowed to take another leave soon. He spent many hours a day writing long love letters expressing his innermost thoughts along with hopeful expectations of their future life together.

General Cleburne, often referred to as the "Stonewall of the West", was a dedicated hardworking soldier who had not taken any leave for the previous three years. In March, he applied and was granted his second leave of the war to return to Mobile to ask Susan to marry him. This time Susan accepted. He remarked, "After keeping me in cruel suspense for six weeks, she has at length consented to be mine and we are engaged." A cruel destiny awaited; Susan was never to see Patrick again!

They wrote frequent love letters that both sustained and enhanced the romance during their separation. Susan wrote to Patrick at least twice a week and always wrote a draft copy before sending on the final version. Patrick's letters, never shared with anyone, did not survive.

In the fall of 1864, just before the start of the Tennessee Campaign, Cleburne went to General Hood to ask for a furlough so that he and Susan could be married. Hood told him that the request would have to be denied for the time being because the army was soon to be on the move. Susan was greatly disappointed when she learned that the wedding would have to be postponed and Cleburne himself was probably sadder than he ever let anyone know. Ever the dedicated warrior however, his thoughts prior to the battle that was to take his life turned very patriotic; "If this cause that is so dear to my heart is doomed to fail, I pray heaven may let me fall with it, while my face is toward the enemy and my arm battling for that which I know to be right."

Late in the afternoon of December 5, 1864, Susan heard a boy shouting the news, "Big battle near Franklin, Tennessee! General Cleburne Killed! Read all about it!" She fainted and went into a state of shock for several days followed by a period of deep mourning. Many of the general's personal effects were sent on to her—his dress sword, sword belt, a captured battle flag, and other items of his apparel.

Like numerous other victims of this war, Susan overcame her grief and, in 1867, married Captain Hugh L. Cole, a confederate veteran. But within a year, tragedy struck again and Susan died suddenly. She is buried in Magnolia Cemetery in Mobile, Alabama.

Major General Patrick Ronayne Cleburne became the highest-ranking foreign-born (Irish) officer in the Confederate Army. He distinguished himself as a superb combat officer. He was the first to suggest that slaves be recruited to fight for the Confederacy as a condition of their freedom. He was killed in the battle of Franklin in November 1864.

Maria Louisa (Louise) Garland Longstreet

"Devilishly Pretty"

Courtesy Mrs. Jamie Louise Longstreet Peterson

As the daughter of General John Garland and Harriett Smith Garland, Maria Louise had numerous opportunities to meet young officers, which eventually included Lieutenant James Longstreet from South Carolina. Born on March 6, 1827 in the Minnesota Territory, she is described as slender, petite, and quite attractive. Another officer admirer, who characterized Louise as "devilishly pretty," claimed that she and her sister were the most attractive girls in the entire state of Missouri.

James was born on January 8, 1821, to James and Mary Ann Dent Longstreet. Born in South Carolina, he spent most of his boyhood yeas in Georgia. His father was a successful, but not rich, cotton farmer. Growing up on the farm, James became strong and lean, enjoying the out-of-doors. His mother was a cousin in he Dent family; the same family of Julia Dent Grant.

She met Lt. Longstreet when she was visiting her father at the Jefferson Barracks. She was a seventeen year old beauty; he was 23. During a long and chaste courtship, the two finally embraced for their first kiss only when James was about to be transferred. He departed for duty in the Mexican War, and she did not see him again for three years. Upon his return in March 1848, they were married at her parents' home in Lynchburg, Virginia. At the candle-lit ceremony, her sister Bessie attended the bride while all of the groom's men were military.

Shortly after their marriage, James started receiving choice assignments that were attributed, with bitterness by some of his fellow officers, to his well-connected father-in-law. And his commanding officer. The two weathered such criticism and continued to be popular with the officer cadre at all his duty assignments.

Later that summer, when Julie Dent and Ulysses Grant were married in St. Louis, the Longstreets were among the guests. James and Ulysses had been best friends at West Point, and Julie and James were distant cousins. The two couples maintained a lifelong friendship.

The marriage eventually produced 10 children, only five survived into adulthood. First, in 1853, William died. Memorializing his death, Louise wrote: "He gave thee, He took thee, and He will restore thee. For death has no sting since the Savior hath died." These were to be prophetic words as Harriett died in 1860 followed by the death, within one week, of three others, Mary Ann, James and Gus, in 1862. All were victims of scarlet fever. But these children did not receive a funeral and were noy buried in 1862, but entombed until 1972. It was then that James bought a marker for a grave for the children. Dan Paterson, the Longstreet's great grandson, researched this matter with the cemetery and shared it with us.

Their marriage was reported to be a happy one, but it is difficult to obtain any reliable insight into the true state of their affairs. Letters were burned in a fire and Longstreet did not discuss family matters in his war memoirs. While stationed at Fort Bliss, Texas for four years, Louise, as the commander's wife, became the focal point of the military community's social life. She reported that these were the happiest four years of their marriage. When James decided to resign from the U. S. Army and join the Confederates, he and Louise bid farewell to their extended family at Fort Bliss. Anticipating the violent drama that lay ahead, it was a difficult parting for all.

During the war Louise stayed home raising their remaining children, but she did visit James at Fredericksburg in 1862. James met her at the train station with an ambulance to which the driver had attached sleigh bells making for a romantic winter drive. Louise stayed at the Hamilton house, about one mile from James' duty station, and they were able to spend each evening together. Otherwise, Louise spent many lonely, uncomplaining nights awaiting word of James' safety.

Shortly after the Battle of Chickamauga 1863, Louise announced the birth of their sixth child, a boy whom she and James named Robert Lee Longstreet. When he wrote to the celebrated Commander of the Army of Northern Virginia announcing that they had so named their son, Lee reportedly was very pleased.

During the Battle of the Wilderness in 1864, James was accidentally severely wounded by his own men. He was first taken to Charlottesville, then Lynchburg to the home of Louise's relatives, John and Caroline Garland. Louise and the children soon joined him there where she was able to share nursing duties with Caroline. He never fully recovered from the severity of this wound, which caused him great discomfort for the rest of his life.

In February 1865, Union Major General Edward Ord and Longstreet met to discuss prisoner exchange; a meeting that also included Julia Grant's brother John. Ord brought up the possibility of ending the war with a negotiated peace settlement between Lee and Grant. Since Julia Grant and Louise Longstreet were friends and James and Julia were cousins, Ord thought that perhaps they could help to bring the two sides to the table. Longstreet discussed the idea with his superiors, Jefferson Davis and Lee, and a dispatch was sent to Lynchburg requesting that Louise come to Richmond. On March 3rd Grant received a dispatch from Lee asking if there was "the possibility of arriving at a satisfactory adjustment of the present unhappy difficulties by means of a military convention." He added that he was authorized to do whatever such a convention might advise. Grant responded, "I would state that I have no authority to accede to your proposition for a conference on subject proposed. Such authority is vested in the President of the United States alone." Louise returned to Lynchburg disappointed.

After the war, the Longstreets' first settled in Lynchburg where the Garland clan welcomed them. From here, James went on to New Orleans hoping to find a way to earn a living and to find suitable living arrangements for his family. They enjoyed New Orleans and participated in the city's elite social life.

James' old commander, Robert E. Lee expressed a concern about how James was going to prepare his war memoirs since he had lost the use of his right arm. He suggested, "Can you not occupy your leisure time in preparing your memoirs of war . . . Mrs. Longstreet will act as your amanuensis [an assistant who takes notes and writes instead of the principal] . . . you must present my kindest regards to Mrs. Longstreet." James came to follow this advice years later.

Initially, the post-war years treated the Longstreets kindly. His business prospects did well, and he also maintained his friendship with his old friend Grant. In 1869, he attended Grant's inauguration and soon found himself nominated for the position of surveyor of the post of New Orleans with an annual salary of $6,000 a year—a substantial sum in the postwar years.

Acceptance of this position coupled with his decision to become a Republican and his advocacy of Negro suffrage lead to the outcry that he had deserted "The Cause". Some ex-Confederate officers, chiefly Jubal Early and John Gordon, held him personally responsible for Lee's defeat at Gettysburg. Louise realized that James' friendship with Grant was responsible for this unjustified attack on his reputation by hard core Southerners. But they continued to be welcomed in the north where they often visited while James was conducting business or attending postwar meetings and reunions. There is no record that Louise ever entered into any public discussion on these issues.

In April 1889, their home in Gainesville, Georgia was destroyed by fire; all of James' wartime correspondence and souvenirs were lost. Having no insurance, they were forced to live in farm out buildings for some time.

Ten months later, after a lingering illness, Louise died of throat cancer at the age of 62. Over a 40-year span, uncomplainingly, she had borne 10 children, grieved over the loss of five of them, spent months separated from her husband while dreading news of his fate. She was the epitome of the dedicated Civil War wife. The aging warrior had lost his long-time mate, and he would mourn her deeply.

Helen Longstreet

In 1887, seven years after Louise's death, Longstreet married Helen Dortch. She was 34, he 76. The old soldier was taken by this attractive, vivacious young lady, but the difference in their ages reportedly caused embarrassment and dismay for his children. She had been a classmate of one of Longstreet's daughters. The union lasted seven years until his death in 1904 when he turned to her and said, "Helen, we shall be happier in this post."

As the attacks on her husband's loyalty to the Southern cause continued and he became too enfeebled to respond, Helen took on the defense of his tarnished reputation. Her work was eventually published in several newspapers, but not until after his death. Her efforts were important in securing his name as a great Confederate leader. It must have been a source of great satisfaction and pleasure when President Theodore Roosevelt wrote her a letter in 1904 that stated; "Not only must Americans hold high the memory of your husband as one of the illustrious captains of the Civil War, but they must hold it high particularly because of the fine and high-souled patriotism which made him, when the war ended, as staunchly loyal to the Union as he had been loyal to the cause for which he fought during the war itself."

Helen had many careers including librarian, reporter, free-lance writer, and editor. Her last reported job was working in the Bell Aircraft factory in Atlanta in 1943. She commuted to her job on the day shift in her Nash coupe dressed in all black (slacks, sweater & visor cap) and white socks. She was 80 years old at the time. She proudly claimed, "I am going to assist in building a plane to bomb Hitler . . ." In 1962, at age 99, Helen was the oldest living widow of a Civil War officer.

Making Bombers for World War II

Life Magazine 9/43

She delighted in telling two stories that her famous husband frequently told on himself.

He once went to Chicago to help with the unveiling of a Confederate monument. Upon arriving he found that his room would cost him $50 a night. After determining that this fee was too great for his budget, he decided to check out and go home. The hotel attendant informed him that he was a guest of the hotel at no charge. Although pleased with this news, he was too proud to return to his room and left for home anyway.

Later, he was a guest in New York to celebrate Grant's birthday. By this time he was nearly deaf, but had taught himself to respond in kind when others laughed and applaud. He could not hear any of the speakers, but one seemed to elicit a roaring response from the audience, so he joined in with gusto. After the crowd had quieted, he turned to his dinner partner, Union General Dan Sickles and asked him what the uproar was all about. Sickles said the speaker had just paid him a grand compliment.

Lt. General James Longstreet, Lee's "War Horse", had major roles in the battles of Manassas, Fredericksburg, Gettysburg, Chickamauga, The Wilderness and more. He was second in command in the Army of Virginia. And was Lee's most trusted subordinate. He died in 1904, the last of the of the Confederacy's senior officer.

Susan Elston Wallace

"What I have of success, I owe to her"

One can easily envision a young Lew Wallace walking pass the baronial Elston mansion in Crawfordville, Indiana and being fascinating by the splendor he saw. Perhaps he even got a glimpse of the pretty young girl that grew up in that house. Susan Arnold Elston was born on Christmas Day, 1830. Her parents, Isaac and Maria Aiken Elston, were wealthy and prominent members of Indiana society. Her father was a successful merchant who had made sound financial investments and his palatial home was a testament to both his influence and affluence.

Susan had blue eyes, wavy hair, a flashing wit, and a beautiful singing voice. Her mother, seeking the best possible education for her daughter, sent her to a boarding school in Poughkeepsie, New York. Early on, she was to demonstrate intellectual acumen and a deep curiosity about the world around her. Lew's family pedigree was also impressive. His father, David Wallace was a West Point graduate and was active in Indiana politics where he served as Lt. Governor, Governor and Congressman. He later became Judge of the Indiana Court of Common Appeals.

Wallace first met the 17-year-old Susan at a social function held at the Elston mansion in 1848. But he was only one of many who were seeking her hand—a group that included a lawyer, a businessman, an elderly "man of leisure," and a preacher. He saw her as a charmer who possessed the beauty of promise in her features. In his autobiography, Wallace had set down his hopes and aspirations in a wife rather pompously and dramatically: "She is waiting for me somewhere in the cool shadows of tonight, and I wait for her. She will love me and I shall make her famous by my pen and glorious by my sword."

By the spring of 1849, Susan and Lew were formally engaged. But, like most young lawyers, he was busy traveling the legal circuit from town to town and they waited three years before they were married. Although his law practice was prospering, her parents still had objections to the match. Some of these doubts were overcome, when Lew became a local hero as he climbed onto the burning roof of an Elston neighbor's house to help put out a fire. His heroism won both parental approval as well as Susan's admiration.

In May 1852, Susan and Lew were married in Crawfordsville. Their honeymoon included a visit to his family's homestead where she delighted everyone and made a particularly favorable impression on Lew's father.

In 1853, Henry Lane Wallace was born, their only child. Later in life, Henry would become his father's business agent.

By 1856, Lew had been elected a state senator and was a natural choice to help organize the Montgomery Guards, a volunteer militia infantry company. Susan wrote the unit song, "Song of the Montgomery Guards." When hostilities broke out five years later, Lew was commissioned a colonel and appointed commander of the 11th Indiana Volunteers.

His performance at Fort Donelson earned him a second star making him the youngest Major General in the army. However, that spring his reputation suffered greatly at the battle of Shiloh. On the first day his division was stationed north of the main army at Crump's Landing. A series of contradictory orders from General U. S. Grant forced him to countermarch his command and thus delay his arrival on the main battlefield until the fighting was nearly over. Although he redeemed himself on the second day, a scapegoat was needed for the near disaster of the first day and the role fell to Wallace. In spite of many fervent efforts to clear his name, he was never to return to front-line action with the

Union Army. He was pretty much ostracized and, except for his brief moment of glory at Monocacy, was left alone in Baltimore, until the end: a Major General without a major command.

Wallace would go on to serve his country in many ways and with the publication of his novel *Ben-Hur*, become a world-renown author, but he never fully recovered from the stigma of Shiloh. Evidence of how this impacted on his relationship with Susan is lacking but it can be assumed that she provided both solace and understanding as he attempted to work his way through this disturbing event. In a letter to Susan written over 20 years later, this proud man was still reflecting on the exasperation and ignominy associated with the events of April 6, 1862: "Shiloh and its slanders! Will the world ever acquit me of them?"

Note: Lew and Ann Wallace would have been pleased with the article by Gloria Swift, "Honor Redeemed: Lew Wallace" that appeared in the January 2001 issue of the *North and South* magazine.

Sometime in early April 1862, Susan and her sister traveled to Washington and were visiting with the President when news arrived from the front that General Wallace had been killed at the Battle of Shiloh. Both were shocked. Then a second message was received clarifying that the dead general was H. H. L. Wallace and not Lew. The two were rejoicing that their loved one had been spared when President Lincoln took them up short reminding them that the dead man "was somebody's Wallace wasn't it?"

Lincoln gave Wallace a second chance when he appointed him to command VIII Army Corps headquartered in Baltimore, Maryland. Fortune intervened in the form of a Confederate Army commanded by General Jubal Early who was planning to attack Washington, D.C. Wallace met Early's forces at the battle of Monocacy on July 9, 1864 and delayed the enemy long enough for Grant to send help and the Nation's capitol was saved.

In 1878, Lew was appointed Governor of the Territory of New Mexico, and the Wallaces moved to Sante Fe. In his official capacity, he was involved in the trial of Henry McCarty—the notorious Billy the Kid. The legendary outlaw threatened the Governor proclaiming that he would ride into town, hitch his horse in front of the governor's palace, and shoot Lew Wallace. As a precaution against this threat, Susan closed "the shutters at evening so the bright light of the student's lamp might not make such a shining mark of the governor . . ."

The Sante Fe of 1878 left much to be desired by way of living accommodations including the mud-built "palace" that was their home, as well as the food, climate, insects, and dust. Susan adjusted somewhat and later was able write little travel sketches for the *New York Tribune* and *Atlantic* magazine in which she presented the city in a favorable light. "It is invested with indescribable romance, the poetic glamour which hovers about all places to us foreign, new and strange," she wrote.

In 1881, Lew was appointed Minister to Turkey and Susan accompanied him. It proved to be a most unfortunate decision as she suffered severely from seasickness and ship conditions in general. After a home leave, Lew prepared to return to Turkey, but Susan turned down another ocean voyage. During his second tour of duty in Constantinople in unaccompanied status, the Sultan reportedly offered him the services of a Circassion girl to alleviate his loneliness. Gossip relative to the Sultan's gesture apparently reached Susan who was not pleased. Lew's reaction is unknown.

In 1885, as he prepared to leave his diplomatic post and close out his public service, he yearned only to study and to write, "to bury myself in a den of books . . ."

Today, Lew Wallace is remembered neither for his military exploits nor his diplomatic service but as the author of his great novel, Ben Hur. In dedicating the book to Susan, he incautiously inscribed it: "To the Wife of My Youth." This obscure use of words caused some women to assume Mrs. Wallace was dead and resulted in several marriage proposals. Susan suggested that future editions include the proprietary phrase, " . . . Who Still Abides With Me." Lew went on to write many other books with varying degrees of success, but none matched the over-whelming reception of Ben Hur.

Susan was the author on her own right and Lew contributed illustrations. During her lifetime, she published six books: *The City of Kings, The Storied Sea, The Land of the Pueblos, Along the Bosphorus and Other Sketches, The Old Oak Chest, The Repose in Egypt.*

Eventually, Lew became bored with the lecture circuit and longed to settle down. They spend their last years together in Crawfordsville, Indiana, where Lew built their retirement home, fondly called "The Study." Today it is known as the Lew Wallace Study and Museum.

He died on February 15, 1905. Susan followed two years later on Oct 1, 1907. They are buried together at Oak Hill Cemetery in Crawfordsville, Indiana.

Over their years together, through many difficulties and separations, Lew developed great admiration and deep respect for Susan. After 50 years of marriage, he expressed it this way in his life's story: "I have been subject to her and her gentle soul has controlled me, and bent me to her wishes, but unselfishly, and always for my own good, and always so deftly that I was as one blind to the domination." He added, "What I have of success, all that I am, I owe to her."

Lew Wallace was the youngest Major General in the Army when he fell from grace at the Battle of Shiloh. He redeemed himself at Monocacy in 1864. He served as Governor of the Territory of New Mexico and as U.S. Minister to Turkey after the War. And, of course, he wrote *Ben Hur.*

Ellen Ewing Sherman

"Love Suffereth All"

Ellen Boyle Ewing was four years old as she watched her father walk up the hill towards the house hand-in-hand with a slender redheaded 9-year-old boy who bore the unlikely moniker of Tecumseh Sherman. From his birth family he had also acquired the equally peculiar nickname of Cumpy or Cump, which he preferred. Sherman was leaving his birth family because his father, Charles Robert Sherman had died prematurely and left his mother Mary Hoyt Sherman unable to provide for the nine surviving children. It proved to be a most fortunate choice of an adopted family. Thomas Ewing, a close friend of the Shermans, was one of Lancaster, Ohio's leading attorneys. Maria Boyle Ewing, the adoptive mother, was a devout Catholic who insisted that young Tecumseh be baptized into her faith and given the Christian name of William, thus overcoming the heathen appellation chosen by his natural parents.

As a substitute family, the Ewings were hard to beat. Thomas Ewing would provide the political clout necessary for Cump to matriculate at West Point; new brother Philemon would become his closest friend during his last years in Lancaster; a second Ewing brother Hugh would be his best companion in later years and finally, foster sister Ellen would become his wife.

In their late teens, Sherman went off to the U. S. Military Academy and Ellen attended a Catholic girl's school in Somerset, Ohio. The relationship matured over the next few years, as both were consistent letter writers.

Thomas Ewing was a prominent and wealthy lawyer, a U.S. Senator from Ohio, and the nation's first Secretary of the Interior in the Taylor administration. He was not overly enthusiastic about the evolving relationship between his oldest daughter and his adopted son. He wanted Ellen to be provided with all the comforts due her station in life and feared she would be unhappy living the vagabond existence of an Army wife.

Young Lieutenant Sherman was assigned to duty in Florida and California, their love continued to mature sustained by their written correspondence. He spent much of his free time reading and rereading the classics hoping Ellen would also acquire the habit.

Ellen was often ill with various ailments. At one point she wrote him that he might consider marrying another women since she was in such poor health.

But these difficulties were overcome and they were married on May 1, 1850. The wedding was a huge social affair in the nation's capitol with President Taylor, his entire cabinet, Daniel Webster, and Henry Clay among the 300 distinguished guests. The bride carried a bouquet given to her by Henry Clay. The newlyweds honeymooned in Baltimore, New York City, and Niagara Falls.

It was an auspicious beginning but recurring problems about his occupation, his religious beliefs, and where they were to live remained. Ellen, no doubt sustained by her family, wanted Cump to leave the army, become a practicing Catholic, and settle in Lancaster, Ohio. He, in turn, would become willing to forgo the military, approached the religious issue with deep misgivings, and was reluctant about settling in Lancaster so close to the dominant albeit benevolent control of Ellen's father. On the religious issue, Cump believed that Truth was his religion and he rejected many Catholic doctrinal points that Ellen wanted him to accept. He did, however, promise to try to examine "with an honest heart and a will to believe, if possible" her Church's theological principles. This avowal, coming from a man who was "not scrupulous in matters of religion," did not bode well for Ellen's hopes.

In 1850, Sherman was ordered to St. Louis while Ellen stayed behind in Lancaster to give birth to their first child, Minnie, in January 1851. Mother and new daughter joined him for a while in St. Louis until he was transferred to New Orleans in October. Once again he made this trip alone as Ellen was back in Lancaster preparing to deliver a second daughter in November. She was christened Mary Elizabeth in honor of Sherman's mother but was always called Lizzie.

In 1853, Sherman resigned his commission and shortly thereafter he, Ellen, and 10-month old Lizzie sailed for San Francisco where he took a job managing a bank. Prior to their departure, the usual conflict about leaving home ensued and was partially resolved when she agreed to accompany him but left little Minnie home with her grandparents. But Ellen, hopelessly homesick and missing Minnie, was far from satisfied with the Golden West.

"I would rather live in Granny Walters cabin [in Lancaster] than live here in any kind of style." she complained. In June1854, she gave birth to William (Willy) Tecumseh Sherman but her homesickness persisted and in the spring of 1855, she left her family behind and returned to Lancaster to visit with her parents. He wrote to update her on Lizzie and Willy, saying that they are "very fat." Willy was gaining weight, "wanted to be carried about", and "tyrannizes over me." Ellen rejoined the family and in October 1855 a second son was born named Thomas Ewing Sherman (Tommy). It was a happy and joyful event and, after one of their best Christmases together, the Shermans looked forward to a more promising future.

It was not to be as the bank managers in St. Louis ordered the closing of Cump's San Francisco branch in April 1857. As the California coastline receded on the boat trip back East, he was bitterly disappointed not only in the failure of his banking career but also in leaving a state that he had grown to appreciate. His high hopes for the future seemed to be fading fast in spite of all his efforts. Ellen, for her part, was pleased to be leaving and looked forward to returning to Lancaster and reunion with her family.

He once again avoided employment in his adopted father's salt works in Ohio by joining up with Tom and Boyle Ewing in a Kansas real estate and law business. This venture quickly lost its appeal and he began seeking ways in which he might return to the Army. His mood is captured in a letter he wrote Ellen in 1859, wherein he bemoaned his fate as a "vagabond "and had given up trying to" struggle against my fate." In early 1860, Sherman was hired as Superintendent of the Louisiana Seminary of Learning and Military Academy. He was well suited for the job, and the school offered to build him a house. He looked forward to having his family join him and seemed to be back in control of his life. And then the war broke out.

For most of the next 6 years, Ellen remained in Lancaster where the last of her six children were born: Eleanor Mary (Elly) in September 1859 and Rachel Ewing born in July 1861.

Sherman served as a brigade commander in General McDowell's ill-fated debacle at Bull Run in July 1861. Although his performance earned him modest military recognition, he was badly depressed with the overall outcome and the panic that characterized the retreat. Letters to Ellen during this time were so alarming that she offered to bring the children and come to Georgetown hoping to provide some solace. This sharp reversal of her normal homebody attitude was a most positive and loving gesture on her part. Cump advised her to stay home believing her presence would set a bad example toward his troops. Here he was admitting that their marriage was to be in part sacrificed to the war and her place was in Lancaster with her family.

When his old friend Major General Robert Anderson, the hero/martyr of Fort Sumter, offered him a command in Kentucky, he accepted. After a short visit home, he went to Louisville. In October he suddenly found himself in command of the Department of the Cumberland when Anderson was relieved of that duty due to poor health. Ill equipped to cope with such responsibility, his pessimism when assessing the military situation facing his command drove him to make unrealistic demands for more troops; pleas that always ended with increasingly alarming predictions relative to the state of affairs in Kentucky. His paranoiac and increasingly erratic behavior generated whispers of possible mental instability. When this news reached Ellen, she persuaded her brother Phil to accompany her to Louisville in an effort to calm her husband. Her weeklong visit did little to relieve his unstable mental condition. Ellen noted that his subordinates expressed grave concern about his behavior and confided that he paid little or no attention to them or to anyone else and scarcely answered questions unless it was absolutely vital. He considered that the whole country was irrevocably ruined and "desolation was at hand."

When Sherman was finally relieved of command by his friend General Henry Halleck, Ellen arrived, unescorted, to take him home to Lancaster for a 20-day leave hoping he could pull himself together. The Ewing family closed ranks around their troubled warrior. Thomas Ewing used his influence in Washington and Ellen wrote directly to the President seeking his help in defending her husband "from his enemies" who she pointed out had plotted against him. Her total and unremitting commitment to his cause culminated in January when she accompanied her father to plead his case with President Lincoln personally and to smooth over his poor relations with Secretary of War Stanton.

Returning home, she developed an interest in the war, which she pursued with the same determination that she applied to her principle concerns: religion and family. She aided charitable causes that benefited the soldiers. The war came to be intertwined with the spiritual in her mind. In the words of Sherman biographer, Lee Kennett, "The Confederacy was a manifestation of the anti-Christ, an instrumentality of the Prince of Darkness;" she sometimes referred to Jefferson Davis as, "His Satanic Majesty."

Eventually, Sherman's depression started to lift, and the stories about his insanity began to fade. General Halleck once again placed him in command of troops and the gods of war sustained him further by uniting him with a western theater general who would become his great friend and advocate, Ulysses S. Grant. As his appreciation for Grant's military prowess increased, his confidence both in himself and in the Union cause grew accordingly. His fortunes were shifting, and Ellen's steadying and loving support during his time of crisis had earned his undying affection and gratitude. Finally, he was a man on his way.

Promised help from Grant did not arrive in time to prevent Sherman's command from being badly mauled at Chickasaw Bayou, but this loss was soon overshadowed by the euphoria that swept the nation on news of Grant's marvelous victory at Vicksburg. In August, with Vicksburg secured, he acceded to Ellen's request to bring the children to visit. He was delighted to see them all. Nine-year-old Willie was particularly favored by being dressed in a Union sergeant's uniform and, thus attired, assisted his father in reviewing the troops. In September, Sherman was ordered to Chattanooga and planned on taking his family as far as Memphis. Enroute, however, tragedy struck when Willie succumbed to dysentery and malaria. Both parents were shattered.

In July 1864, while her husband was conducting his historically famous march from Atlanta to the sea, Ellen was going through a transformation that led to a decision to finally leave her father's house and move the family to South Bend, Indiana. Although Sherman was initially annoyed by this added expense, he was secretly proud of her determination to break with Lancaster and her father's influence. After thirteen years of marriage and seven children, this move acknowledged that Cump and not her father was the most important man in her life.

She was proud that Sherman was gaining fame as a national hero but she also missed him. He was fighting his way to Savannah in early December when baby Charles died. Facing this death alone, she reminded Cump that the deaths of Willie and Charlie were a lesson to us of "the vanity of human glory."

From war's end until 1873, they lived in St. Louis where Sherman was in Command of the Division of Mississippi. With Grant's ascendancy to the White House, he arranged for his friend to replace him as Commander of the Army. The family moved to Washington where they occupied Grant's old home at 2051 I Street, NW. In his elevated status he traveled extensively throughout Europe where he was wined and dined with all the ceremony due a national hero. Ellen stayed home and became increasingly withdrawn from all social activity. Unable or unwilling to accommodate herself to the classic social role expected of Victorian wives, she found her life's fulfillment in attending to her family duties.

As she increasingly gave way to various infirmities and old age, her daughter Minnie was pressed into service as hostess for various social functions and daughter Lizzie was relied on to manage household affairs. Increasingly irritated with her attitude, Cump was forced to attend to his many social obligations as a Washington celebrity alone.

As the nation's second greatest soldier, Sherman thrived on the attention that fame brought. He enjoyed his frequent travels as well as the theater and dinner parties. Ellen's reclusive behavior rendered him a virtual bachelor socially, and he enjoyed the attentions of other woman who were attracted to him. He exchanged copious letters with Mrs. Charlotte Hall between 1877 and 1890. He had what was called a "quasi-bohemian alliance" with sculptress Vinnie Ream. In the summer of 1880, upon the death of his longtime aide Joseph Audenreid, he developed a strong attachment to his widow Mary who "threw herself at him." He allowed himself to be seen in public with both these woman, which might very well indicate that there was more flirtation than intimacy in these encounters. Those who knew him well declared his attraction to Mary Audenreid in particular was more a father/daughter relationship than anything else.

Ellen never confronted him about these romantic liaisons. Her decision to destroy Mary Audenreid's letters to Cump seemed to have been motivated by religious scruples rather than jealousy.

When her father died in 1873, Ellen edited a 290-page memorial that glorified his memory, which was published by the Catholic Publication Society. Liddell Hart has suggested that she saw in her father the kind of husband she wished she had married concluding that, "Mrs. Sherman was born to verify that love suffereth all."

In the spring of 1878, Thomas Sherman had completed his studies at Yale and his father was busy making arrangements for him to join a St. Louis law firm. In May, however, the senior Sherman was stunned when Tom announced he was abandoning the law and would become a Jesuit priest. In anticipation of his father's unequivocal rejection of such a career choice, he would study abroad thus somewhat minimizing the impact of this rejection of parental plans for his life. Sherman was enraged, labeling his son a "deserter" and saying, "he is absolutely lost to me." It took him three years to come to terms with Thomas' decision, thus making reconciliation possible.

By 1887, Ellen's health had continued to decline and she suffered her first heart attack followed by a fatal one in 1888. Cump was downstairs in his study when her heard the nurse calling him to come quickly. He rushed up two flights of stairs saying as he went: "Wait for me Ellen, no one ever loved you as I loved you." His desperate attempt was in vain; she died before he could reach her.

When Sherman himself died in 1891, a deathbed tableau heavy with ironic overtones was played out. He had lost his ability to speak but was conscious when his children summoned a priest who administered the Roman Catholic rites of extreme unction. Ellen would have been pleased.

William Tecumseh Sherman gained fame as commander of all troops in the Western Theater during the Civil War, becoming best known for his "March to the Sea". When Grant became president, Sherman was appointed to full general and Commander-in-Chief of the Army.

Lucy Webb Hayes

"Justice and Mercy Should Go Together"

Rutherford B Hayes Presidential Center

As the wife of Rutherford B. Hayes, Lucy was one of the most popular and respected of the Presidents' wives. Her keen interest in public affairs, her valiant and courageous volunteer work during the Civil War, and her untiring, loyal support of her husband's career truly earned her the title of "First Lady". She came to the White House well respected and left it loved by the entire nation.

Lucy was born in Ohio in 1831, the daughter of Dr. James Webb, a physician who devoted much of his time and fortune to buying and liberating slaves. He died of cholera in 1833, leaving Maria Cook Webb, Lucy's mother, with a comfortable legacy that permitted her to raise their children with cultural and educational advantages. Maria, a woman of deep religious convictions, also possessed unusual strength of character. Lucy was raised in a happy home, attended the best schools, and received a strong moral upbringing.

When Lucy's two brothers went off to Ohio Wesleyan University, Maria purchased a cottage on the college grounds where the family lived while the boys attended classes. As a result of these arrangements, Lucy was able to study along with her siblings. This exposure prepared her well for her eventual attendance at Wesleyan Female College in Cincinnati. Her mother sent her to Wesleyan not only to garner the finest education available but also to keep her isolated from the many young men admirers who were increasingly attracted to the pretty 16 year old. One teacher described her as tall, erect, and majestic. With her graduation at 18, Lucy was destined to become the first wife of an American president who had a college degree.

Rutherford Hayes was a promising Cincinnati lawyer when he started making regular visits to the Webb home. Lucy's mother was impressed with the young suitor and did much to move the courtship along to a favorable conclusion, as did his sister Fanny. He confided in his diary, "I guess I am a great deal in love with_____ . . . Her low sweet voice . . . her soft rich eyes . . ." Love continued to bloom and the two were married in 1852; Lucy was 22, Rutherford 30. After a month of marriage he said she was a better wife than he could have hoped for. Her deep religious opposition to slavery was contagious, and Rutherford soon adopted similar convictions.

Fanny Hayes was very close to her brother and soon became Lucy's best friend. Fanny's death in 1857 during childbirth was a severe blow to them both. Between 1856 and 1873, Lucy gave birth to eight children. Five lived into adulthood. She followed her mother's example by encouraging proper behavior and stressing educational achievements while nurturing a family life of peaceful serenity.

At war's onset, Rutherford and Lucy's brothers joined the Union army—the Webbs as doctors and he as a major in the 23rd Ohio infantry regiment. His willingness to volunteer was fully endorsed by his wife. Her enthusiasm for the Union cause was demonstrated early in 1862, when Lucy and her mother treated four wounded Union soldiers who were stranded in Cincinnati. Lucy demonstrated early on that it was important to treat the wounded on both sides with compassion. She spent two winters in camp with Rutherford and volunteered to work with the wounded in a hospital in Frederick, Maryland.

When Lucy made a flag for the 23rd Ohio, Rutherford wrote her a thank you note mentioning that the flag was proudly being flown in front of his headquarters. Her reaction to this news was swift and certain as she told him the flag was meant for the men not the headquarters' staff. Furthermore, he was to tell the troops how dear they all are to us on the home front. Rutherford complied making arrangements to formally present the flag to the regiment at the next dress parade.

In 1862, Rutherford was wounded during the battle of South Mountain. Lucy received the following terse telegram from Washington, D.C. "I am here. Come to me. I shall not lose my arm. Rutherford." Finding friends to take care of their children, she left on the first stagecoach. In Columbus, her brother-in-law, William Platt, met and accompanied her on to Washington. Here she searched frantically and in vain for her husband at the City's many hospitals. At one hospital she noticed several wounded soldiers with "23" designation on their caps. When she called out, "23rd Ohio?" the wounded soldiers recognized her as the commander's wife. Much to her relief she was informed that Colonel Hayes was being cared for at the Rudy house in Middletown, Maryland. Soon Lucy and William were on their way to Frederick where her brother Joe Webb, a doctor in the 23rd Ohio regiment, met them and took them on to Rutherford. Dr. Webb's expert treatment is credited with saving his brother-in-law's arm.

After the Battle of Cedar Creek in 1864, the Cincinnati newspapers carried a story that Rutherford had been killed. Her uncle hid the papers from Lucy until a telegram came with news that he had been wounded, but not seriously, and was safe. For his performance at Cedar Creek, he was promoted to brigadier general.

As matters in the Shenandoah Valley calmed, Lucy decided to move to West Virginia to be with Rutherford. She quickly installed herself as a glorified "den mother" to the men, caring for them when ill and listening to their grievances. When her sewing machine arrived from Ohio, she helped patch up uniforms. There are a number of stories testifying to the favorable impact her presence had on the unit. One involved a young soldier who was lamenting that he could not mend his torn blouse. He was recommended to a "woman" in General Hayes' tent that sewed for the regiment. Without fanfare, the tattered garment was returned the next day mended and folded. Such attention to the needs of her husband's soldiers earned her the name, "Mother Lucy." Many no doubt remembered her kindness years later as they voted for Rutherford at the polls.

Lucy joined with the rest of the nation in expressing the joy in the fall of Richmond and Robert E. Lee's subsequent surrender at Appomattox on April 9. The sorrow attendant to the assassination of President Lincoln five days later quickly squashed this exuberant mood. She wrote, "From such great joy how soon we are filled with sorrow of the endless talk of forgiveness & taking them back as brothers. Justice and Mercy should go together." Perhaps anticipating her husband's admonition of her choice of words, she added, "Now don't say to me Ruddy that I ought not to write so."

Lucy accompanied General Hayes to the Grand Review of the Union Armies on May 23 and 24, 1865. She was thrilled to see the victorious armies but wrote, "While my heart is filled with joy at the thought of our mighty country . . . the sad thought of the thousands who would never gladden home with their presence made the joyful scene mingled with so much sadness . . . that I could not shake it off."

Rutherford's exemplary military performance earned him election to Congress as well as three terms as Governor of Ohio. These years provided Lucy with valuable experience in public life in both Washington and Columbus. She devoted a large amount of her time to various state charities and was one of the founders of the Ohio Soldiers' and Sailors' Orphans' Home. She was also active in several church activities.

Rutherford B. Hayes followed U. S. Grant to the Presidency in 1876, elected by the margin of a single electoral vote. As she watched her husband take the oath of office her beautiful and serene face impressed even the most cynical critics. Her role as First Lady was characterized by a dedication to humanitarian causes. And her knowledge of political issues, her intelligence and cheerful spirit made her a charming hostess.

As a member of the National Women's Christian Temperance League, she refused to permit alcohol to be served in the White House. Her choice of beverage earned her the nickname "Lemonade Lucy"; a title that was not always kindly meant and was used only after she left the White House. Her only exception to abstinence was when foreign dignitaries were visiting and expected wine to be served with dinner. When the Lucy Hayes Temperance Society of Washington got wind of this indiscretion, her name was removed from the Society's official letterhead.

When Congress decided that the annual Easter egg-rolling activity did too much damage to the Capitol lawn, she had the event moved to the White House lawn thus preserving the popular event that is still enjoyed today. On their fiftieth wedding anniversary, Lucy and Rutherford renewed their wedding vows in a White House ceremony. It is reported that she wore her unaltered wedding gown for the event.

With the help of the newly invented typewriter, Lucy wrote about her wartime experiences as well as her life in the White House where she became the first president's wife to be called First Lady. Her writings are included in the book, *First Lady* by Emily Greer. Her writings can be viewed on the White House website.

After the presidency, Lucy and Rutherford retired to their Spiegel Grove home in Fremont, Ohio, an occasion marked by cavalry escorts, marching bands, and a torch—light ceremony. They lived an active but relaxed life and had the leisure to enjoy family and friends. In retirement, Lucy took a great interest in the house with its gardens and the many animals she cared for. As she aged, Lucy was plagued with severe headaches and gastric disorders that severely curtailed her activities. She continued to serve as president of the Woman's Home Missionary Society until her death in 1889. Rutherford outlived her by four years.

Thousands lined the streets to watch her funeral procession, which included an honor guard from the 23rd Ohio marching on each side of the hearse. Her contributions to the country in war and peace were glowingly reflected in newspaper obituaries nationwide.

General Rutherford B. Hayes entered the army as a major and eventually earned a rank of brevet major general. He displayed creditable leadership as a division commander in the Valley in 1864. He resigned his commission to take a seat in Congress in June 1865 and went on to become the 19th President of the U.S.

Catherine Mary Hewitt

The Girl He Left Behind

Major General John F. Reynolds was killed on July 1, 1863 during the opening moments of the Battle of Gettysburg. As the fallen First Corps commander was being attended by his aide Major Riddle, he found a medallion on a chain around his neck and a ring on his finger inscribed "Dear Kate." His West Point ring was missing. Who was the mysterious Kate? His friends assumed that she was Reynolds's lover, but no one had heard of her, not even his close-knit family.

Her name was Catherine Mary Hewitt. John had met her aboard a steamer bound from San Francisco to New York, a four-week journey. At the time, Kate was 24 and he had just turned 40.

On September 15, 1861, John stopped in Philadelphia to visit his sister. At that time, he also proposed to Kate and both marked the event by exchanging rings. Over the next year, Kate wrote him several letters sealed in wax and imprinted with his West Point ring.

Reynolds went home on leave in the winter of 1863 to visit his family as well as his beloved and at that time they set July 8 as the date to announce the engagement to his family. He died at Gettysburg one week shy of his formal betrothal to Kate.

The metal coffin containing the fallen hero arrived in Philadelphia at the home of his sister on July 3. Later that morning, Kate came to view the body. She was led upstairs where she wept uncontrollably on her knees occasionally remarking, "Dearest, how can I give you up?" She removed the West Point ring from her finger and placed it in the coffin beside the body taking away the Catholic medal the General had worn around his neck.

Kate then revealed that she and John had an agreement: in the event of his death, she would enter a Catholic convent, for life without him would hold no interest for her. On July 12, eight days after the funeral, she entered the convent of The Daughters of Charity of Emmitsburg, Maryland, and a short 10 miles from the site of his death. She was given the name Sister Hildegarde and was assigned to teach.

The Reynolds family remained in touch with Kate, hoping to include her as a member of the family and she met in subsequent years with the General's faithful aide Sgt. Veil. Her correspondence with the family lasted until 1868 when she left the convent in poor health and vanished. All attempts to find her failed.

An highly esteemed Union corps commander, Major General John F. Reynolds was in charge of three corps on the first day of the battle of Gettysburg. As he was placing his infantry units in line, a Confederate sharpshooter killed him.

Almira Russell Hancock

"The Most Beautiful Girl in the West"

Library of Congress

It was 1848, the Mexican war was over and a group of young officers were roving about St. Louis accompanied by the regimental band serenading the local ladies when someone in the party announced that one particular lady, "the most beautiful girl in the west" was staying nearby. The group marched to the new destination, appropriate music was offered, a shutter was slightly opened and a white object was thrown out. The object, a kid glove, was handed to Lt. Hancock. The lady's name was Almira Russell.

Later in the year, Major Don Carlos Buell, a West Point friend, introduced Hancock to the owner of the white glove, the golden haired beauty who was the daughter of a prominent merchant named Samuel Russell. Little time was loss in the wooing process and on January 24, 1850, the couple married. Almira was eighteen and Winfield seven years older. The ceremony was marred by violent weather that extinguished all the lights on three separate occasions. The bride was later to recall that the weather might have produced a sensation of impending evil in the minds of some in attendance but for the newlyweds, life was "so full of promise as to defy the predications of the universe."

A prominent resident of St. Louis recalled Almira as being a "woman of fine physique and striking comeliness of face, an accomplished musician, sparkling in conversation, ready with gems of repartee, and bounteously endowed with a kind and generous nature, she was universally admired and beloved."

Winfield Scott Hancock was quickly transformed from his old life of casual nocturnal adventuring to that of a happily married man. His marriage to Allie Russell was a contract for life and she in turn provided strong and unyielding support for her soldier husband. On October 29,1850, Allie gave birth to a healthy son who was given the family name, Russell.

In the ensuing years, the Hancocks were assigned to southern Florida at the time of the Seminole Wars of 1856-57. On February 24,1857, a daughter named Ada Elizabeth was born at Ft. Meyer. Shortly thereafter, the couple moved to Fort Leavenworth, Kansas during the controversy surrounding that state's admission to the Union in a free or slave status. It was here during the time of "Bleeding Kansas" that the Hancocks were exposed to the sectional disunity that was sweeping across the country. Winfield was next posted to Southern California. Allie, anticipating the arduous trip with two small children, had doubts about accompanying him. Her memoirs recalled she was approached by then Major Robert E. Lee who advised her that her place was at her husband's side. Lee closed by saying," Now promise me that you will not permit him to sail without you". Consequently, shortly after Winfield arrived in California, he immediately took leave to return east to accompany his family to his new post. On April 4, 1859, Winfield, Allie, Russell and Ada left New York City for the long and arduous trip across the Isthmus of Panama and on to California.

As Chief Quartermaster for the Los Angeles settlement, Hancock found it necessary to entertain some Sioux Indian chiefs while they were en route to Washington to visit President Pierce. Allie recalled that they quickly became fascinated with the piano and she was requested to provide some music. Impressed, the chiefs immediately began negotiations "to purchase the 'big Captain's' squaw along with the music table." When in the face of the beads and blankets that were proffered in exchange, the "big Captain" rejected their offer; they left the house with great indignation.

News of the attack on Ft. Sumter reached California on April 24, 1861. Shortly thereafter, the U.S. Army officer cadre in Los Angeles, their emotions wrenched and deeply divided by state loyalties, prepared for the long journey back east to join the respective warring sides. George Pickett, Richard Garnett and Lewis Armistead sought out Winfield's advice. It was unyielding: "I shall not fight upon the principle of state-right, but for the Union, whole and undivided."

In a scene later made famous by Michael Shaara's book, "Killer Angels"— Allie was to recall vividly the last time the group met at the Hancock home the night prior to departure. General Sidney Johnston prevailed upon his wife to sing one or two of the old songs, "Mary of Argyle" and "Kathleen Mavourneen."

"All were endeavoring," she recalled, "to conceal, under smiling exteriors, hearts that were filled with sadness over the sundering of life-long ties, and doubts as to the result of their sacrifice."

Newly promoted Brigadier General Hancock was to emerge from General McClelland's ill-fated peninsular campaign with an enhanced reputation. Allie was proud of her husband's new grade and credited McClelland with having helped make it possible. He fought at Antietam in the fall of 1862, at Fredericksburg in the desperate assault on Marye's heights in December and, following the Rebel victory at Chancellorsville in May of 63, led the rear guard that protected the Union withdrawal.

Meanwhile, Allie had taken a house in Washington in anticipating the need to help nurse Winfield should he become wounded. She recalled that "depression and apprehension filled the hearts of all" as Union armies seemed to go from defeat to disaster leading up to the Battle for Gettysburg in July of 1863.

She was visiting her mother in St. Louis when she received a telegram from Gettysburg on July 3rd informing her: "I am severely wounded, not mortally. Join me at once in Philadelphia." The wound, a Minie ball imbedded in his thigh that was not cut out till two months after the battle, was a source of constant agony throughout the remainder of his life. The convalescence was prolonged, as Hancock was not able to return to active duty as Commander of the Second Corps till March 23, 1864. The 2nd Corps fought in the Wilderness, at Spotsylvania, earning Hancock his second star, suffered terrible losses at Cold Harbor in June and finally, after the fight at Hatcher's Run on the Petersburg front, Hancock was relieved as head of the 2nd Corps and assigned to recruiting duties.

In July, Allie and Winfield were reunited when he assumed command of the Middle Military District with headquarters in Baltimore. During this time, Allie remembered a "very charming and most interesting" trip to the Gettysburg battlefield including a visit to Big Round Top.

After a brief post-war tour in the Missouri department, the Hancocks left St. Louis for New Orleans where Winfield commanded the Louisiana and Texas

Military District. Shortly thereafter, Hancock's Democratic Party-States-Rights political orientation ran afoul of the Reconstruction attitude prevailing in Washington and when General Grant countermanded one of his orders, his request to be relieved was honored.

In 1875, Winfield was briefly considered as a gubernatorial candidate for his home state of Pennsylvania. However, on March 28, 1875, the Hancock's' daughter, Ada died at the young age of eighteen. Allie recorded "the seclusion, gloom and depression" This tragedy curtailed all interest in politics for a while.

After having been denied the Democratic Party presidential nomination on several previous occasions, Winfield finally succeeded in 1880 only to lose to Republican James Garfield in one of the closest national elections in American history. Allie recorded that when he awoke at 5 a.m. the day after, she told him, "It has been a complete Waterloo for you." "That is all right," he replied, "I can stand it," "and in another moment he was again asleep."

Life was catching up with Winfield and Allie. In April 1883, Allie's mother died. A year later, shock and bereavement struck again when their son Russell died at the age of thirty-four. Finally, Hancock himself was approaching death's door. On the morning of February 8, at about 6:15, as Allie looked on, he struggled to speak to her: "O, Allie, Allie! Myra! Good—" He was unable to finish.

In 1887 Allie wrote a somewhat sentimental view of her life, which did add some useful glimpses into their relationship. Winfield's death left Allie in difficult financial straights. An effort was started to raise a fund that would allow her to live in some comfort. Eventually, some $55,000 was collected from various subscribers. She lived in a donated house in Washington until 1891, when she left to spend a year in Dresden, Saxony. Upon returning, she lived in New York City until she died on April 20, 1893. She is buried in the Russell family plot in St. Louis.

Major General Winfield Scott Hancock was a veteran of the Mexican and Indian Wars before becoming an effective Corps commander in the Union Army. His performance at Gettysburg drew high praise. He later ran unsuccessfully or President of the United States.

Ellie Junkin Jackson

"My sister is going on our honeymoon"

Daniel Henry Hill, later to become Lt. General D.H. Hill of the Confederate Army, was instrumental in bringing about the courtship of Ellie Junkin and Thomas (Stonewall) Jackson. Hill was a professor at Washington College in Lexington and was consulted by the president of Virginia Military Institute concerning a faculty vacancy. He recommended his friend Thomas Jackson and the two developed a strong professional and social relationship. The Hill's were a socially active couple and invited young Jackson to many of their parties. It was at one of these occasions that he met Ellie Junkin, whose father was President of Washington College.

Ellie was sweet, intelligent, and reserved. Thomas was a somewhat uninspired suitor, however, and after two years of repeated visits to the Junken home, Ellie called off the courtship. But, Thomas had fallen in love.

Eventually, with the help of Hill and his wife Isabelle, the relationship was rekindled. Hill in particular became exasperated with Jackson's behavior toward Ellie, declaring at one point that Thomas' problem was that he was in love and simply refused to admit it. Eventually, the reluctant suitor finally summoned the courage to approach the Hill's one night and asked Isabelle if she would tell Ellie of his love for her. It was in this roundabout way that the protracted courtship ended in a proposal of marriage. Like most events in his life, Jackson never did things the easy way. They were married on August 4, 1853 and accompanied by Ellie's sister Maggie, left for an extended wedding trip.

The newlyweds returned to Lexington to live with Ellie's parents. The marriage was destined to be a short one for Ellie died due to complications of childbirth on October 22, 1854, barely a year after their marriage. Thomas' grief was inconsolable. He is said to have made daily visits to Ellie's gravesite for a long time thereafter. He eventually went off to Europe for a while and returned much composed as well as having regained some of his old confidence.

Mary Anna Jackson

Sing to Me of Dixie

Mary Anna Morrison was slightly built, good looking, and cheerful. A minister's daughter from North Carolina, she was a graduate of Salem College— which still continues to honor her with scholarships in her name for young ladies. Her father was the founder and first president of Davidson College. Her mother, Mary Graham was the daughter of General Joseph Graham and the sister of William Graham, governor of North Carolina, U.S. Senator, and secretary of the Navy in President Fillmore's administration. She was well traveled and had many important social contacts, which she eventually made available to her daughters. The Morrisons lived on a plantation in rural Lincoln County where they raised six daughters and four sons.

The summer of 1853 had been an eventful one for the young Mary Anna. First she enjoyed a trip to Washington, D.C. where she had tea at the White House with the president's daughter, Mary Fillmore. Later, she and her sister Eugenia visited her older sister in Lexington, Virginia, where they crossed paths with Jackson, a professor at Virginia Military Institute. She recalled that her first impression was that he was friendly and cordial and that he appeared to be very soldierly—erect in bearing and striking in his military dress with flashing blue eyes.

As their friendship deepened and Thomas' intentions became clearer, Anna realized she was in love. In the spring of 1857, with the full blessing and support of her family, the two were engaged. The courtship was to provide Thomas with an opportunity to demonstrate a sentimental side of his personality not normally associated with the stern "Stonewall Jackson" image. He wrote many letters to Anna expressing how, "In my daily walks I think much of you. I love to stroll . . . after the labors of the day are over, and indulge feelings of gratitude for all the sources of natural beauty . . ." In May 1857, he revealed " . . . When in prayer for you last Sabbath, the tears came to my eyes and I realized an unusual degree of emotional tenderness." And again in June, "I never remember to have felt so touched as last Sabbath the pleasure springing from the thoughts of payers ascending for my welfare from one tenderly beloved."

The letters had their desired effect and they were married on July 16, 1857 and went on an extended honeymoon. This time the bride's sister did not accompany the newlyweds.

Anna and Thomas were religious, attending church, observing the Sabbath, and teaching Sunday school. Sunday was set aside exclusively for worship. No business or socializing was conducted and no books were read except the Bible. They also taught a Sunday school class for Lexington's Negro children. In 1858 Anna gave birth to a girl named Mary. Her subsequent death three months later caused both parents great distress.

After Abraham Lincoln's election and the probability of secession loomed, the Jacksons felt certain that Virginia would not follow those southern states that had already succeeded. Both were equally sure, however, that if Virginia did chose to leave the Union, they would stay loyal to their native state.

As the war evolved and Thomas' heroics at the battle of Manassas earned him the *nom de guerre* of Stonewall, Anna found herself to be much celebrated as the wife of a famous confederate general. Her efforts urging Thomas to take leave to spend some time with her repeatedly failed as he informed her he could not leave his command. She made frequent visits to the front visiting him at Winchester, Manassas, and Fredericksburg. She was always warmly welcomed at the front by her husband's officers and troops.

These excursions often proved to be difficult and disagreeable, thus demonstrating much grit and determination on Anna's part. The trip to Winchester from North Carolina, for example, involved both a train and stagecoach ride during which she lost her trunk and reached her destination exhausted, disoriented, and lonely. She arrived about midnight and all she could see were groups of soldiers standing around. One particularly seedy—looking warrior seemed to be staring at her when he abruptly came over and kissed her on the lips. She gratefully fell into her husband's arms. She later wrote that she enjoyed "three blessed months in Winchester." She taught Thomas how to sing Dixie by repeating the popular anthem over and over until he got it. They shared many chuckles over these "Dixie lessons." In Winchester, Anna repeatedly tried to learn of the general's battle plans, but the secretive Stonewall resolutely resisted her as he did most of his subordinates.

On her visit to Manassas, the scene of Thomas' initial triumph as a field commander, Mary Anna insisted upon being shown the entire battlefield, a request Thomas responded to with enthusiasm.

Thomas was delighted when Anna brought along their new daughter Julia to visit him at Fredericksburg where the child was christened. During this visit she was struck with awe when she met General Robert E. Lee. She wrote, "I was met by a face so kind and fatherly, and a greeting so cordial, that I was at once reassured and put at ease."

The visit was cut short when signs of a coming battle emerged. She left for Richmond to the roar of cannon fire; the battle of Chancellorsville had begun. Here she anxiously awaited word that all was well and that she would be allowed to return. It was not to be as Jackson was mistakenly severely wounded by his own men and it was far too dangerous for her to come to him. After a two-day wait, her brother, Captain Joseph Morrison arrived to escort her to Guiney Station where her husband lay dying. His condition was so grave that she was initially denied permission to see him. When he improved slightly she went to him displaying a sad demeanor, which prompted Thomas to ask her to cheer up and get rid of the long face. She read to him from the Bible and sang some of his favorite songs. When the doctors told her his condition was hopeless she insisted that she be the one to tell him. When told that death was imminent, he responded, "I prefer it."

Lover, husband, companion, and father of her child gone, Anna grieved her loss. She needed to face the full reality that she was now a widow with a five—month-old child. Escorted by men from her husband's brigade, she and Julia left for Charlotte, North Carolina.

As the Stonewall legend grew, southerners coming to pay tribute would stand in line for hours for a glimpse of Anna. As a symbolic sentiment to this adulation for her husband, she placed his saddle on the post in her front hallway so visitors could touch it.

A quiet and gentle lady, she enjoyed a spicy story, a good joke, and was fond of appropriate entertainment. Her knack of putting everyone around her at ease and of keeping her troubles to herself added to her popularity. Anna had complied with Thomas's insistence that she invest their money in Confederate bonds that became worthless after the war. Partly to alleviate her financial distress and partly as a tribute to her gallant warrior, she wrote a book entitled "*The Life and Letters of Stonewall Jackson*" published by Harper & Brothers in 1892.

Anna was often invited to speak at southern veterans' conventions and was always greeted with enthusiasm and the inevitable "rebel yells." She once attended a reception elegantly attired in a beautiful gown wearing an old soldiers hat rakishly perched on her head almost covering her face. When asked about her curious choice of headdress she replied that the hat belonged to an old soldier who had asked her to wear it in his honor.

She lived to be hosted by five U. S. Presidents—Arthur, McKinley, Theodore Roosevelt, Taft, and Wilson. At a White House reception, while attending a DAR convention, she was introduced to President McKinley who grasped both her hands and said, "Mrs. Jackson, I have long desired to meet the widow of the great Stonewall Jackson." Turning to his wife he continued, "Dear, this is Mrs. Stonewall Jackson." To which, the gracious first lady responded by offering Anna the bouquet of violets she was holding and inviting her to be a part of the receiving line. She declined stating that she preferred to join her friends in the East Room.

Anna outlived her husband by 52 years dying at age 84 in 1915. All businesses in Charlotte were closed during the funeral. She is buried in Lexington next to Stonewall's grave and monument.

When President Theodore Roosevelt visited Charlotte, he made his apologies to the governor, the mayor, and other dignitaries who came to meet him, saying, "As I got off the train I was greeted by one citizen of North Carolina whose greeting pleased and touched me more than the greeting of any other man could have touched me. I was greeted by the widow of Stonewall Jackson."

Major General Thomas (Stonewall) Jackson was an effective Corps Commander of the Confederate Army. He distinguished himself at Chancellorsville when he marched around the right flank of the Union Army in a surprise move. Shortly thereafter, he was mistakenly shot by his own men.

Kitty Morgan Hill

Impervious to Danger

Photographs of Kitty Morgan clearly show the lovely, fragile, doll-like features that earned her the nickname Dolly. She was part of a prominent Lexington, Kentucky family that included a sister and six brothers. Both girls eventually married Confederate Generals and all six brothers fought for the Confederacy. Her brother John H. Morgan rose to the rank of general. All six were eventual wounded: two fatally. All six were also prisoners of war at some time during the conflict—truly a "border state" family that had given all for the Rebel cause.

Kitty's first marriage in June of 1855 was to her cousin Calvin McClung, a prosperous St. Louis merchant. He was fond of calling her his "Kentucky Babe," claiming that he had tamed her of her crude country ways. Bragging to his family that she had not spoken a harsh word since leaving Lexington he boasted: "Quite a reformation." Calvin died suddenly at an early age leaving Kitty a young but well-off widow.

Meanwhile, her second husband and love of her life, Ambrose Powell Hill was actively but unsuccessfully in search of a wife. He first pursued Miss Emma Wilson, a beautiful Baltimore classmate of his younger sister. They were engaged when he was 25, but the marriage never took place. He then found that he was courting the same woman, Miss Ellen Marcy, as his West Point classmate, George McClellan. When Ellen rejected McClelland and accepted an engagement ring from Hill, the couple set about persuading Ellen's parents to accept the arrangement. It was not to be as Mrs. Marcy learned from an unknown source that her daughter's suitor had contracted gonorrhea while a cadet at West Point. Under heavy parental pressure, Ellen returned Hill's ring. Twice engaged, twice rejected.

But Hill remained determined to find a mate that would have him. He wrote his sister "You know that I am so constituted, that to be in love with someone is as necessary to me as my dinner, and there is a little siren that has thrown her net around me." The "little siren" was the young widow, Dolly McClung.

Hill was attracted to her almost immediately and married her on July 18, 1859, at her parents' home in Lexington. The bride's wedding dress was later made into a battle flag for Hill's Virginia Regiment.

Dolly was described as sparkling, vivacious with blue eyes and chestnut hair that fell to her waist. Her lovely speech was accentuated by a singing voice akin to a nightingale. She was also opinionated, out going, and wealthy. Her fiancée described her to his friend George McClellan, "She is young, 25 years 7 months, gentle, amiable, yet holy and sufficiently good looking for me. I know you will like her." He fancied the nickname Dolly and used it throughout their marriage.

Following the wedding, they settled in Washington, D.C. There, his modest army pay augmented by Dolly's income, they led an exciting social life surrounded by many new friends and were accepted in the finest social circles.

In May 1860, Hill attended the wedding of his friend George McClellan to his old flame Ellen Marcy. Full satisfaction with his own married life allowed him to overcome any residual bitterness about having lost Ellen to his old roommate.

The Hills had four daughters. Henrietta (Netty) died early in December 1862. Then came three more girls, Frances (Russie), Lucy, and Ann. Only Frances and Lucy were to survive into adulthood. Ann (nicknamed "AP") was born two months after her father's death. She died in 1868 just short of her third birthday. Her godfather was General Robert E. Lee.

By the outbreak of the war, the Hills had become almost inseparable. Dolly's commitment to stay close to her warrior husband lead to much worry and concern on his part. She appeared to be impervious to danger and repeatedly ignored Hill's admonitions to stay away from the front. When a rumor surfaced that Union General Philip Sheridan was expected at a nearby hotel, legend has it that she snuck across Union lines in an effort to get close enough to spy on the Yankee cavalryman. She was discovered and fled as the enemy opened fire.

General A. P. Hill was killed at the Battle of Petersburg in 1865. The brief war-ravaged marriage was reputed to have been a happy one. Years later, their daughter recalled that her parents had loved deeply, and the union had been an ideal one. She remembered that her father was a man of fine traits, courteous, possessed of a wonderful sense of humor—a true southern cavalier. It might have been a display of this sense of humor that moved him to wear a red shirt into battle, claiming that if he were shot his men would not see the blood.

Embittered by the war and its terrible aftermath, Dolly refused to support any of the "Lost Cause" sentiments that sprouted up during this time. She also dropped the nickname Dolly and returned to being called Kitty.

She remarried in 1870 to a Louisville doctor, Alexander Forsyth. They had two children prior to his death in 1875. Kitty lived for 45 more years, dying in Lexington on March 20, 1920.

Her grave marker reveals no mention of her life as the wife of the heroic Confederate General A. P. Hill; it is marked simply "K. Forsyth."

Lieutenant General Ambrose Powell Hill was regarded by General Lee as a fine combat officer. His timely arrival at Antietam earned him Lee's respect. He led the Confederate Third Corps at Gettysburg, the Wilderness, and Petersburg, where a union straggler killed him.

Ellen Mary Marcy McClellan

"How did Lincoln greet you—the old reprobate!"

Picture History

The study of Ellen and George McClellan yields an interesting paradox. On one hand they were both alert and active participants in the affairs of the nation during the early days of the War and yet, they both seemed at times to face the evolving events the country was experiencing with a certain air of unreality and detachment. They sustained one another in the belief that George was the victim of a conspiracy that extended from the President and his minions on the one hand to Robert E. Lee and a Confederate phantom army whose size and formidableness was constantly growing on the other. Together, the couple created and nurtured a great disillusionment—the nature of which was to bring about George's downfall.

The first daughter of Captain Randolph and Mary Amelia Mann, Marcy was named Ellen Mary, but was usually called Nellie. She was born on May 17, 1835 in Green Bay, Wisconsin where her father was serving at the time and was often nursed by an Oneida squaw who carried her around in a blanket on her back, papoose style, and taught her some simple words of her native language.

Captain Marcy, a Massachusetts native, brought a strong Puritan background to family affairs that included early rising, politeness towards others, and controlling one's temper. He also counseled that children should be wary of trusting their own judgment in making decisions, instead turning to their elders for council confident that they would not be deceived. It was hoped that, so guided, Ellen and her younger sister "Fannie" would grow up to make their parents proud and thus be ready to take their place in privileged society. This also required a solid Christian education and, to that end, Ellen attended the Hartford Female Seminary. She matured to be a beautiful and graceful young woman with a poise and carriage that had been carefully nurtured by thoughtful parenting and proper schooling.

While Ellen's parents were busy preparing for her debut into high society, George was already "to the Manor born." His father was a Yale and University of Pennsylvania educated physician who was also the founder of Jefferson Medical College in Philadelphia. His mother, Elizabeth Steinmetz Brinton, came from a distinguished Philadelphia family. She was a woman of high cultural refinement who saw to it that her children received the best education possible which included the study of Latin, French, and the classics. They were comfortable in the upper levels of Philadelphia society and counted people such as Daniel Webster as a friend.

At the time George met Ellen, he had graduated from West Point second in his class and was doing well in the army as an engineering officer. Her parents liked George and were disappointed when Ellen turned down his proposal of marriage. He waited 8 years for her to change her mind. In the interim, George maintained a steady correspondence with Mrs. Marcy, sending her news of his activities along with occasional gifts. But Ellen was looking elsewhere and finally fell in love and agreed to marry Ambrose Powell Hill, George's West Point roommate, whom George considered "one of my oldest and best friends."

Her parents were adamantly opposed to the engagement. Captain Marcy warned his daughter that marriage to a line officer would mean a "life of exile, deprivation and poverty" and forbade her to have any correspondence with Hill. As the pressure from her parents mounted, she reluctantly broke the engagement. One roommate's loss became the others gain.

Ellen was not lacking for suitors. Between 1855 and 1859, she had no less than nine proposals of marriage including one from the superintendent of West Point, soon to be General John Barnard. George reentered the quest for her hand in 1859. Actually he had never entirely given up having stayed in touch with Mrs. Marcy through the intervening years. When he lamented in 1856 that Ellen was indifferent to him, Mrs. Marcy reassured him and encouraged him not give up hope.

George decided to leave the army in 1856 and accept a job as chief engineer for the Illinois Central Railroad. It was an excellent move paying him double what he had been making in the army. He was entitled to a private rail car along with a home on Lake Michigan.

Ellen and her mother were invited to travel in his private car for a trip to Green Bay. They also accepted an invitation to stay at his lakeside home. Impressed with George's affluence and thoughtfulness, Ellen finally accepted his proposal and they secretly engaged. When the news was made public in January, it was highlighted in the social columns of both the New York and Philadelphia papers. The couple married on May 22, 1860 and the wedding guest list included all the "proper" people, including General Winfield Scott.

Ellen gave birth to two children Mary (May) McClellan in October 1861 and George Jr. in November 1865. Both children survived to adulthood.

President Abraham Lincoln named George General-in-Chief of the Army in the fall of 1861. He accepted and with great enthusiasm and organizational skill, went about making an army out of a group of loosely organized volunteer units. His efforts resulted in greatly improved moral and nurtured high expectations as to how the army would perform in actual combat conditions.

But McClellan was unable to achieve on the battlefield what he had done so well on the drill field. He was accused of being too slow in moving his army into action. When his superiors in Washington kept urging him to move with greater speed, he resisted, continuing to claim that he had too few troops or that conditions were not yet favorable to insure victory. The press, becoming increasingly frustrated with his inactivity, began calling him "Mac the Unready" and "The Little Corporal of Unsought Fields." The President had his own homespun way of describing George's lack of initiative, "He's got the 'slows'". He reacted to such slurs with insolence and bitterness.

Ellen was furious when President Lincoln ordered a portion of George's army be transferred to General Pope to fight the second battle of Manassas. This decision came after George had extricated his army from the Virginia peninsular following a halfhearted attack on Richmond. Ellen expressed her outrage in a letter to George insisting that if Pope was placed in command over George, that George had no choice but to quit the army. She concluded that she would use all of her influence to make him quit because she could not "endure the idea of your being under that puppy."

Later that month, Ellen wrote to George that she needed to know what happened when he visited Washington. "Write me explicitly," she pleaded. She wanted to know how Lincoln had treated him—"How did old Lincoln greet you—the old reprobate!" It seemed that by the summer of 1862, wherever the McClellans turned, they were surrounded by implacable foes that bore them ill will. No one seemed to be exempt from the ever-growing list of evildoers.

That the President was their prime antagonist was well evidenced in their correspondence. He was described alternately as an "old reprobate," an "idiot," or a "well meaning baboon." As one contemporary wit observed: McClellan found Lincoln as being unworthy of McClellan.

Secretary of War Edwin Stanton was the "vilest man I ever knew" George wrote. In one dispatch during the Seven Days battles he wrote Stanton "If I save this army now, I tell you plainly that I owe no thanks to you or any other persons in Washington. You have done your best to sacrifice this Army." Only the prudent intervention of the telegraphic office clerk prevented this venomous passage from being sent on to Washington, an event that would have resulted in his dismissal.

Secretary of State William Seward and General-in-Chief Henry Halleck also came under attack. McClellan's paranoia was becoming contagious.

Ellen, ever ready to amplify his delusions in her adoring letters, told him she almost wished that he would march on Washington and frighten those people. "I long to have the time come when you can have your revenge" against the "mean and contemptible" actions of the administration.

Finally, after remarkable forbearance, the President had had enough and, following a lackluster performance at the battle of Antietam, "Little Mac" was fired as commander of the Army of the Potomac.

As a private citizen George went on to be very successful in business. Ellen, continuing her role as dutiful and supportive helpmate, was regarded as a charming and thoughtful hostess.

George ran for president on the Democratic ticket to unseat Lincoln in 1864, but was not successful. His party was badly split on the issue of slavery, and George did not want to deal with it as an issue. Ellen's views on slavery are not available, but since they agreed on all other matters, it might be assumed that she was sympathetic with George's position.

After the election, the McClellans went on a two-year European tour. By this time George was quite wealthy and they enjoyed seeing Europe in style. Ellen became the "first lady" of New Jersey in 1877 when George was elected governor for a three-year term.

Feeling the need to spend "a few weeks at St. Moritz," they went back to Europe 1881. When they returned, they were devastated to find that all their stored belongings had been destroyed in a fire.

In the winter of 1882, they rented a house in Washington at 1730 Massachusetts Avenue and began entertaining officially and privately. By this time their daughter May was a prominent young socialite and George Jr. was a student at Princeton. His son's tutor offered high praise of the senior McClellan calling him possessed of the best manners of any man he ever met.

In October 1885, George never recovered from a severe attack of angina pectoris and, early in the morning of the 29th, he was heard to murmur, "I feel easy now. Thank you . . ." and then died.

After his death Ellen and the two children returned to Europe where she lived as a "*grande dame*" for the next 30 years. She died in her daughter's home in Nice, France in 1915.

General George McClellan was named General-in-chief of the Armies of the United States by President Lincoln in 1861. He brought order to a badly disorganized group of volunteer units. Following the Battle of Antietam, Lincoln dismissed him. He was a successful businessman, but an unsuccessful presidential candidate in 1864

Teresa Baglioli Sickles

The Rapscallion's Child Bride

New York Historical Society

On February 27,1859, Philip Barton Key was lurking outside the Sickles residence off Lafayette Square in Washington D.C. He was attempting to signal his lover, Teresa Sickles to arrange another elicit meeting when her husband, Congressman Dan Sickles spotted him. In a fury, Sickles rushed from his house, ran across the street and shot and killed the ill-fated lover. This impulsive act would trigger one of the most sensational murder trials in the history of the nation's capitol.

Teresa Baglioli was born in New York in 1836. Her family lived in the home of the noted Italian musician and composer Signor Daponti. As a friend, Daniel

Sickles has also lived in Daponti's house and had often cuddled Teresa as a young child. The family was highly upset in 1852 when the sixteen-year-old Teresa revealed she was pregnant and that she and Sickles had been secretly married. At this time, she was a student in a Catholic boarding school and he a successful New York Lawyer. To dignify this embarrassing development, a church wedding was quickly arranged. It became a gala and largely attended affair with the archbishop of New York conducting the ceremony. Their love child, Laura, was born three months later.

One of the most glaring anomalies associated with Victorian morality was that it tolerated great leeway for men to carry on any number of sexual liaisons with almost total impunity; an advantage that Dan Sickles was quick to exploit. One of his earliest affairs was with Mrs. Fanny White, the owner of a New York City bordello, who he once blatantly took on a tour of the New York State Assembly.

When James Buchanan was appointed United States minister to London, Sickles went along as his secretary. Initially Teresa did not accompany him to London over concerns about how the baby might take the trip. Undaunted, Sickles invited his friend Fanny White to accompany him instead. He boldly introduced her to the Queen of England under an assumed name.

Teresa and their child joined him in London several months later and Fanny was shipped home. Teresa quickly became a social celebrity and was invited to balls, receptions, and socials. She, too, was introduced to the queen. One contemporary described Teresa as an Italian beauty, warm, openhearted, and unselfish. Another described her as being " . . . without shame or brain and [having] a lust for men." Still another described her as a lovely creature with delicate features and a sweet manner.

On returning to Washington, she was highly sought in the social circles of the nation's capitol where Dan was now serving as a member of Congress. For six years, her ravishing good looks and charm became a fixture in D.C. social life. The Mediterranean beauty attracted the attention of many men, something her husband encouraged as a means of making important contacts. Even President Buchanan, a bachelor, took an interest in her welfare.

The Sickles lived in a fine house on Lafayette Square adjacent to the White House. They entertained formally every Thursday evening. Teresa was also "at home" to other society ladies every Tuesday morning. The Sickles were clearly living well, beyond the modest salary of a Congressman. Many speculated that his involvement in Congressional affairs was not always ethical. Eventually, when several public funds that he supervised from time to time came up short, no one was surprised. These suspicions of unethical behavior, however, never became a legal problem.

Teresa appears to have been well aware of her spouse's extra marital activities including the notorious Fanny White. Contemporary accounts reported that he also had affairs with several different "Mrs. Sickles" at various rendezvous in

Baltimore and New York. It was also rumored that he had an affair with Teresa's mother; an event, if true, that occurred prior to his marriage to Teresa.

Teresa's motivations for becoming romantically involved with Philip Key are partly understandable. Knowing of her spouse's transgressions, she certainly felt little restraint in pursuing a romantic affair of her own. Sickles had befriended Key, a widower and lawyer, aiding him in attaining a position as District Attorney for Washington during the Buchanan administration. Young Key had previously earned a reputation as a bold, daring, and irresistible lover who had already lost an ear at the hands of an irate Pittsburgh husband who had caught him in a compromising situation with his wife.

Taking advantage of Sickles' frequent absences on out-of-town business, Teresa and Philip had ample opportunity to meet. They developed a signaling system using handkerchiefs and scarves to pave the way for their increasingly frequent elicit meetings. As the affair progressed, the lovers took more risks and finally they were observed together—usually at 383 15th Street where he would enter by the front door—she the back.

When Sickles first heard the rumors, he tended to overlook them in the face of Teresa's strenuous denial coupled with his firm belief that his friend would not betray him in such a manner. Eventually, he received an anonymous letter, which stated in part,

"There is a fellow I may say for he is not a gentleman by any means by the [name] of Philip Barton Key . . . who rents a house . . . on 15th Street btw'n K & L streets for no purpose than to meet your wife Mrs. Sickles. He hangs a string out of the window as a signal to her that he is in and leaves the door unfastened and she walks in and sir I do assure you he has as much the use of your wife as you have. With these few hints I leave the rest for you to imagine."

When confronted again, Teresa admitted the affair. The night prior to the homicide, Dan made her write out a detailed and salacious letter of confession. When queried as to the frequency of her rendezvous with Key, she answered the occasions were so numerous she could not remember. Sickles was furious.

This eventually led to the dramatic encounter at Lafayette Square. Sickles accosted Philip with three loaded pistols: he fired once and missed, fired again and wounded Philip, then, while his helpless friend lay begging for mercy, he fired a third time killing him in cold blood.

While in jail awaiting trial, Sickles was to receive many special privileges including the use of the warden's apartment for entertaining guests. It was during this time that he received a long letter from Teresa that ended with; " . . . . during the first years of our marriage my good conduct did not keep you true to me. Ask in your heart, who sinned first, and tell me, if you will."

Covered in detail by all major newspapers in the country, the trial was protracted and scandalous. *Harper's* described Key's behavior as "a three fold crime—against the women the adulterer misled, against the husband he dishonored, and against the society he threatened to disorganize." Public sentiment ran heavily in favor of the cuckolded husband and he received many letters of support—including one from President Buchanan. They reflected a strong sentiment supporting the view that the murder was the "American Way" to handle such an affront to a husbands honor.

Teresa was badly abused by the press and virtually abandoned by her friends. Her husband, the champion of dual standards, took away her wedding ring and acted like the battered victim. A team of defense attorneys led by James Brady and Edwin Stanton augmented by a group of New York lawyers, prepared his defense using the first successful plea of temporary insanity in U. S. history. After a sensational 20-day trial that titillated the nation with "Glamour, power [and] a whiff of sin", an all male jury acquitted Sickles after deliberating for only one hour. The verdict was enthusiastically celebrated in the courtroom and across the country. Women were not permitted to attend the trial since some of the testimony was deemed to have been too offensive.

Sickles' notoriety and popularity was short lived, however, when he shocked everyone by forgiving Teresa and resuming their former relationship. He professed that the affair had strengthen their marriage and that their love was stronger than ever. With unrestrained audacity he let it be known that he would "strive to prove to all that an erring wife and mother may be forgiven and redeemed." Support for his cause quickly evaporated and the couple was increasingly shunned by Washington society. Teresa eventually moved back to their New York home while Sickles ended his last term in Congress in general isolation.

The outbreak of the Civil War served to rescue Sickles' reputation somewhat. He became a politically appointed general in the Union Army and, as commander of the Third Corps in the Army of the Potomac, lost his leg at Gettysburg. In the role of wounded hero, which he played to the hilt, he was returned into the good graces of Washington society. This rehabilitation did not extend to Teresa. She was never asked to visit him in camp and he continued to isolate her when he left the Army. Later, when he was dispatched on a mission to Columbia, Teresa and their daughter Laura saw him off, but were not invited to accompany him.

After the war he was appointed military governor of the Carolinas while Teresa and their daughter remained in New York. Wherever she went socially, she was ostracized and/or verbally harassed. Sickles was frequently absent for long stretches and she was left to raise Laura alone with some help from her mother.

Teresa Sickles lived out the remainder of her life as a pariah and died a lonely and broken woman at the age of 31. Sickles returned from Charleston for the funeral. The well-attended service was a display of support for the grieving husband rather than any show of sympathy for the deceased. The newspapers covered the funeral in detail but made no mention of the notorious Key affair.

In her teenage years, their daughter Laura became addicted to alcohol and sexual excess. While in Spain, she had an embarrassing affair with a Spanish officer, continuing a life of total dissipation that her father could not control. She died in 1891 in a rented room in Brooklyn. Sickles did not attend her funeral.

Caroline de Creagh Sickles

The Spanish Senorita

In 1869, President Grant appointed Dan Sickles as American minister to Spain. There he married the beautiful and wealthy belle of the court, *Senorita* Caroline de Creagh with whom he was to father two children, George and Ada.

Shortly after their marriage, Sickles started an affair with the deposed Queen Isabella II of Spain. She was an eager partner in the relationship in keeping with her reputation of being sexually promiscuous. Sickles was mocked in the Spanish newspapers as the "Yankee King of Spain."

When Sickles returned to the United States, Caroline refused to follow. Meanwhile, he had taken up with his housekeeper, a Mrs. Elinor Wilmerling. When his wife finally did come to visit him, she stayed in a New York hotel. It was not until his lover-housekeeper, Mrs. Wilmerding, died that Caroline agreed to move into his house.

In 1914, the amoral "American Scoundrel" died. Sickles is the only Corps commander not represented by a memorial statue at Gettysburg. Undaunted, he claimed that the entire battlefield was his monument!

Major General Daniel Sickles was a member of Congress before the war and a colorful and notorious Union commander during the first two years of he war. He lost a leg at Gettysburg and went on to served the U.S. in various diplomatic posts as well as several more terms in Congress.

Flora Cooke Stuart

"Educate the children in the South"

Courtesy of Stuart Hall

Flora Cooke was born in Missouri on January 3, 1836, the daughter of Colonel Philip St. George Cooke, a Virginian and a colorful, accomplished career military officer. Early glimpses described her as accomplished and charming but not particularly pretty. Educated at a private boarding school in Detroit, she met James Ewell Brown Stuart while her father was commander of the 2nd U.S. Dragoons at Fort Leavenworth, Kansas.

From their first meeting she appears to have been smitten by the gallant Stuart and they were married at Fort Riley in November 1855 after a fourteen-day courtship. The marriage was to last a mere nine years, during much of which JEB was away at war. The union would produce three children: Flora, known as Little Flora, who preceded her father in death at the age of 5; J.E.B Stuart, Jr., who was originally named for his paternal grandfather but was renamed after Flora's father turned his back on his native Virginia and remained loyal to the Union; and Virginia Pelham, named in honor of John Pelham, Stuart's 24-year-old artillery commander who was killed in action at Kelly's Ford in March 1863.

Early on Stuart's ability to lead men in the face of danger and adversity impressed his commanders. He was first exposed to war fighting Indians on the plains of Kansas and was seriously wounded in the chest on July,1857 while engaged against the Cheyenne. He wrote Flora downplaying his wound telling her it was not dangerous. His quick recovery bears testimony to his strong constitution and excellent physical condition.

Stuart resigned this commission on May 14, in order to join the Confederacy as a colonel in the 1st Virginia cavalry.

"Marked by showy elegance; splendid" is one definition of dashing, a term often used to describe Stuart. This suited him perfectly. Adorned in a red-lined gray cape, hat cocked to the side in a rakish angle complete with a peacock feather, rich full beard, sparkling blue eyes, a bright yellow sash complete with tassels, he was the epitome of the southern cavalier. People took notice, particularly women, toward which he reciprocated. It is not known how much Flora actually knew about his various and continuing admiration of attractive women. At one time, this interest extended to General Lee's daughter, Mary, who visited him when he was stationed in Fairfax, Virginia. He wrote to Flora saying he hoped she could meet Mary some day. These flirtations seemed to be harmless, as evidence of any impropriety are lacking.

As the war raged on, Flora attempted to stay close to her husband, a task made difficult since JEB was a cavalry commander and on the move much of the time. While he was stationed at Fairfax Courthouse, she rode out to see him daily and, when appropriate, they would take long rides together. But as soon as she heard the firing start she would get tearful and become very concerned for his safety. He did what he could under the circumstances to facilitate her visits saying, " . . . I have a very nice place here for you to visit me . . . I can't promise that you'll see much of your husband when you come and you mustn't say it is cruel in me to leave you at short notice for the imperative calls of duty."

Flora knew, first hand, what it was like to be an Army wife. She was never known to complain, even when he was gone for extended periods of time. However, as the long absence surrounding the Gettysburg campaign wore on she sent frequent telegrams to Lee's headquarters seeking word on his situation. JEB's reaction to these queries precipitated a heated note back admonishing, "Don't be telegramming General Lee's staff or anybody else. If I am hurt you will hear it very soon." Since JEB was already on Lee's bad side over his whereabouts during the first two days of the battle, one might assume that he didn't need any extra attention from his commander during this time of disfavor.

In turn, he was also concerned about her safety. After the battle at Beaver Dam, JEB rode to the nearby home of Col. Fontaine, to be assured that she had not been harmed. Flora was often at his headquarters when he returned and she and other wives arranged parties for the returning cavalrymen. At one such event, she presented him with a Confederate flag she had made. She was to learn later that it had fallen from its staff into a fire. He sent her the damaged remains saying, "I send you fragments. It had waved over many battlefields and if I ever needed a motive for braving dangers and trials, I found it by looking upon that symbol placed in my hands by my cherished wife, and which my dear little Flora (his daughter) so much admired."

When news of Little Flora's death reached him, JEB grieved deeply over the sudden loss coupled with his concern that Flora would have to bear this burden alone. Shortly thereafter, she and little Jimmy (JEB Jr.) were able to visit camp and JEB noted that she was distraught and easy to tears. When General Lee heard that Flora was nearby, he came to offer his sympathy. The German-born General Heros van Brocke noted, "I was touched by the gentle sympathizing way in which he talked with Mrs. Stuart."

During one of their last meetings, Flora was in camp when JEB received a gift of golden spurs from a lady in Baltimore. Apparently, without a jealous thought, she helped him buckle them on. Such evidence suggests that she trusted him completely. In response to some overheard gossip that came Flora's way about some possible impropriety, he wrote her, "My darling, if you could know (and I think you ought) how true I am to you and how centered in you is my every hope and dream of earthly bliss, you would never listen to idle twaddle . . ."

After a hazardous series of many narrow misses, JEB was fatally wounded at the Battle of Yellow Tavern. He struggled to stay alive until Flora could get to him. His comrades made extraordinary efforts to expedite her along her way but it was not to be. He died, on May 12, 1864, just three hours prior to her arrival. His dying words were, "I am resigned, if it be God's will. I would like to see my wife." He also expressed a belief that he would soon be with Little Flora.

Flora kept her promise to JEB that the two children would live and be educated in the south. She supported her family as a teacher and became the head mistress of the Virginia Female Institute in Staunton, which was later renamed Stuart Hall in her honor in 1907.

In 1905,The Virginia Division of the United Daughters of the Confederacy made her their Honorary President.

In their brief years together, he always preferred that she not wear dark clothing, insisting that it detracted from her beauty. Acknowledging that he would not have approved she, nonetheless, continued to wear mourning garments for the rest of her life.

Flora outlived her husband by 59 years dying on May 10, 1923. She was buried with great ceremony beside General Stuart in Hollywood Cemetery in Richmond, Virginia.

Major General James Ewell Brown "JEB" Stuart was an outstanding cavalryman in the Civil War. His daring exploits included riding completely around the Army of the Potomac thus providing General Lee of vital intelligence. He was killed at Yellow Taverns in Virginia in 1864.

Fanny Haralson Gordon

"Bride of the Battlefield"

Hargrett Rare Book and Manuscript Library
University of Georgia

Frances Rebecca Haralson celebrated her 17th birthday on September 18, 1854, by marrying John Brown Gordon. The event took place in the somber environment of her father's bedroom at his Myrtle Hill estate. Hugh Haralson lay on his deathbed; it was his desire to see Fanny get married. Honoring his wish, Fanny and John canceled their plans for a large church wedding and were quietly united at her father's bedside. He passed away within two weeks of the ceremony.

The two had a brief "love at first sight" courtship. In later years John enjoyed teasing Fanny by telling friends that they had been engaged two weeks after they met. When Fanny protested that he was exaggerating, he would ask how long it really had been. This usually brought forth from a smiling Fanny that she thought it had been at least three weeks. This tender vignette is an example of how, early on, the two lovers enjoyed each other and expressed a devotion that was to characterize their married life together.

Fanny's home was in LaGrange, Georgia, but she spent much of her early life in Washington D.C. where her father was a Congressman. She became acquainted with Washington social life and was introduced to many of the prominent personalities of the day. Hugh Haralson served four terms in Congress and chaired the House Military Affairs Committee during the Mexican War.

One can easily image the frustrations her parents experienced as they viewed many of Fanny's youthful activities as less than fitting for an aristocratic southern lady. Her two older sisters carried on with the dignity appropriate to their station in life, but she much preferred the role of a tomboy with tree climbing and riding spirited horses bareback her preferred pastimes. Anticipating the arrival of her father, it was often necessary to call Fanny away from her more athletic antics to avoid his displeasure at her boyish pursuits. She grew up a curious child fascinated by life on the plantation and eager to assist at every task at hand. These childhood experiences would provide her with the knowledge and skills she would need later in life. Despite her rough and tumble early years, she entered her late teens with a reputation of being the "toast of the town." She was pretty, vivacious, intelligent, and charming. A private tutor provided most of her early schooling, but she also acquired a store of practical knowledge that was both varied and profound. She developed a tenacity early on of getting to the bottom of things, a trait that allowed her to pass judgment on the question at hand with authority.

The young married couple lived briefly in Milledgeville where John served as a newspaper reporter but eventually moved to northwest Georgia where he managed a coalmine with his father.

They were living in a mountain log cabin near the Alabama border when war broke out. John had long been an advocate of secession so his decision to enlist was clear. He raised a company of mountain men and offered their services to the governor of Georgia, a bid that was turned down and caused Fanny great indignation since she and other wives had been busy making uniforms for the troops. Eventually the governor of a neighboring state took up the offer and John's men become a part of the 6th Alabama.

Fanny faced a critical decision: Should she stay home with their two boys while John went off to war, or should she place the children with the senior Gordons and go to war with her husband? She chose the latter—as the Atlanta

Journal put it, " . . . to be a heroine at her hero's side." With this unusual decision, Fanny often found herself near the front lines and, at Winchester, was actually in the middle of the conflict. Fanny was not the only wife to follow the Army, but she was one of few who did so consistently.

Although she missed being at Gettysburg and the 1864 encounter at Cold Harbor, she was true to her pledge. She would find housing near the Army encampments that permitted her to be with John whenever possible. Guilt over having neglected her sons was partially alleviated by arranging for them to come to her at times when the Army was resting or regrouping.

Fanny never fully adjusted to the terrors of war, but she did develop the fortitude to endure it. As she wrote John, "Since I began to write the cannons have begun to boom. It is a fearful sound to me, but let us pray, O God, answer the prayers that are filled this day for deliverance." Her daughter Caroline later wrote that he mother was able to overcome her anxiety about the war through the strength and solace she found in her religious faith.

There were many who did not approve of having a wife so close to the front. One who voiced his displeasure was the erasable lifetime bachelor who was also John's commanding officer, General Jubal Early. At one time he issued orders to the effect that wives should be sent away from the Army when new campaigns were about to start, an edict Fanny ignored.

In frustration, General Early said that he wished the Yankees would capture Mrs. Gordon and hold her until the war was over. Word of his pronouncement reached Fanny who waited until she was seated at dinner with Early and some of his officers to tease him about it. He was overcome with embarrassment and, after taking a minute to recover his composure, responded that General Gordon was a better soldier when Mrs. Gordon was around, so she should ignore his orders that wives belonged in the rear. This gallant reply drew a round of applause all around and prompted one witness, General Stephen Davis, to comment, "She had a way with her."

Her continued ability to stay close to her husband rested on two things: first, she never interfered with John's duties in camp, and second, she tried to avoid General Early when he made his inspection tours. Somehow, Early always seemed to find out she was there. Once he saw an unusual wagon parked in camp and asked his quartermaster who belonged to that wagon. When informed that it was Mrs. Gordon's wagon he cursed and commented that he wished his soldiers would keep up with the Army as well as she did.

It was at the Battle of Sharpsburg (Antietam) that Fanny's courage and determination were fully tested. John was seriously wounded when he found himself stationed at the center of the Confederate line on the crest of a hill on the Sunken Road, also known as Bloody Lane. He had promised General Lee that his men would " . . . hold their lines till the sun goes down." However he was hit by five Minie balls early in the battle, the last one a hit to his face. When he regained consciousness he found himself in a nearby barn on a pile of hay. Dr. Weatherly, his long time friend and surgeon, was standing beside him taking his pulse. When he asked the doctor about his chances for recovery, John saw the look of hopelessness on his face.

Fanny was brought to his side while the firing still continued. Suppressing a scream at the sight of him, she started tending to his needs. John wrote in his memoirs that she was told by the doctors to paint John's wound with iodine three or four times a day. John would later report that she painted them three or four *hundred* times a day. He commented later that he owed his life to her incessant watchfulness night and day and to her tender nursing through the weeks of recovery. Fanny later claimed to have her own recipe for recovery—a mighty surge of love and tenderness that kept up his will to live. When Gordon's men heard that Miss Fanny was tending to their General, a tremendous shout came up.

Her early experience as a horsewoman served her well during the war. John, concerned with the quality of the horses Fanny was able to find, gave her a horse that was named Mayre after the battle at Mayres Height in Fredericksburg. Fanny came to be much admired as she strode along displaying her erect carriage and graceful horsemanship. An old soldier, writing to John after the war, closed one letter with a cordial goodbye and a remembrance of Fanny astride Mayre, "I hope Mrs. Gordon is well. Tell her I wish I could see her on her fine horse again. She must not forget me. I am truly yours, R E Lee."

At Winchester, when John's troops were retreating through the town, she pleaded with them to return to the front. One soldier is reported to have responded to her pleas saying, "Come on, let's go back. We can't resist Mrs. Gordon." About this time, John himself came into town and was shocked to see her on the street with bullets flying around. He told her to get off the street and under cover for the Federal troops were right behind him. She asked some men to get her carriage ready and, accompanied by her son Frank and two wounded Confederate officers, barely made her escape. As she fled one end of the town, the Federal cavalry were rapidly entering the other end. She quickly drove her carriage to the rear of General Rhodes division when the alarm was sounded, "Cavalry in pursuit!" Rhodes halted his men and threw them in a line across the road behind Fanny's carriage allowing her to escape.

Fanny did not accompany John when General Lee invaded Pennsylvania enroute to the fateful Battle of Gettysburg. After the momentous three-day struggle he wrote her about the terrible sacrifices the men had made and how grateful he was to have survived unharmed. His brigade had received praise from Generals Early and Ewell but he went on to say that these compliments mattered little to him what did matter was that God had spared him. He consistently referred to his deep love for her and spoke of his "aching heart" at the thought of being separated from her.

Confederate soldiers were fond of Fanny. She was often asked to assist with the wounded and the dying and performed these tasks with great compassion. This heroic behavior explains why both Confederate and Union soldiers came to refer to Fanny as "The Bride of the Battlefield." Over picket lines, gray shared with blue stories about this amazing woman whose youthful beauty and courage were so admired. Northern soldiers home on furlough were known to speak of her in glowing terms, a tribute to southern womanhood.

The following incident attributed to the Petersburg campaign bear eloquent witness to how some soldiers felt toward Fanny. A member of the Stonewall Brigade sent her this note along with some flowers.

Stonewall Brigade—June 5th 1864

Will Mrs. Gordon accept this Boquet (sic) of flowers culled in front by a soldier of this Brigade?

To which Fanny replied:

Mrs. Gordon accepts with pleasure the beautiful Boquet "culled in front" by a soldier of the Stonewall Brigade. It will be preserved and greatly prized as an interesting memento of the deeds of that glorious Brigade in this memorable Campaign. "In the rear." June 5th, 1864.

As the military situation in Petersburg and Richmond began to deteriorate, Fanny was in Richmond about to give birth to their third child. Her condition was such that she was unable to travel, and John was forced to leave her behind. He feared for her safety and hoped that she could be kept out of harm's way. When the Union army entered Richmond and Union General Grant heard of Fanny's plight, he ordered sentries to be placed around the house to protect her. Shortly thereafter the war ended and John returned to Richmond to see Fanny but was met at the door by Union sentries. Telling him that they were there by General Grant's orders to protect General Gordon's wife from intrusion, they denied him entrance. Only when he was properly identified was he allowed access. John was appreciative of Grant's concern for his wife's safety and it led to a lasting friendship between the two. Gordon later served as a pallbearer at Grant's funeral.

It took most of April for the small family to work its way back to Atlanta. They resided in Brunswick, Georgia for a short time and then moved to Atlanta where they built a house called Sutherland. They lived there until 1904 when John died. His fellow Georgians honored him by electing him governor in 1886 and 1888. The also returned him to the United States Senate for three terms in 1873, 1879, and 1890.

Fanny was regarded as a brilliant and charming hostess both in her home state and in Washington. The Atlanta Constitution reported that she " . . . was the best type of southern woman that Washington has seen in many a day . . . cultured, graceful, generous, loyal, tender, brilliant, and winsome." Fanny often accompanied John when he spoke at veteran reunions and was always warmly received.

Their daughter Caroline wrote that her parents were well suited to one another. She claimed that her father had a quick temper but his wrath never fell on Fanny or the children. She also reminisced about evenings at Sutherland when Fanny would play the guitar and sing for the family. The Gordon's had six children: Hugh 1855, Frank 1857, Frances 1863, John Jr.1865, Caroline 1873 and Carolina 1877. Fanny's last child was born at about the same time that Senator Gordon convinced President Hayes to withdraw occupation troops from South Carolina. A delegation of grateful South Carolina women traveled to Washington to thank John and urge Fanny to name her newborn daughter Carolina. Since the Gordons already had a daughter named Caroline, Fanny thought two such similar names might cause confusion. But the South Carolina women persisted and the new baby was christened Carolina, but was always called Lina.

Fanny outlived John by more than a quarter of a century, dying at the age of 93 in 1931 and is buried beside him in the Oakland Cemetery in Atlanta. She had been a member of the United Daughters of the Confederacy and a former president of the Georgia Confederate Memorial Association.

Addendum: In later years, when the state of Georgia dedicated a monument to General Gordon on the grounds of the capitol in Atlanta, daughter Caroline and her family were among the honored guests. Caroline had married a northerner and was living in New Hampshire with her husband and two sons aged 10 and 12. During the ceremony every time the name of General Gordon was mentioned, the enthusiastic veterans in attendance let out a Rebel Yell. The two grandchildren remained respectfully silent. Finally their exasperated mother could stand it no longer and, turning to them, said sternly, "You two Yankees! Why don't you yell?"

Major General John Brown Gordon was regarded by his superiors as an excellent field officer. Although not a West Point graduate, he rose to command half of the infantry in the Army of Northern Virginia. Seriously wounded at Antietam, he survived the war and was elected to three terms as a U. S. Senator and one term as governor of Georgia.

Fanny Shepperd Pender

"Read to the End!!"

William Dorsey Pender first met Fanny Shepperd in 1854 when he was visiting the home of Sam Shepperd, one of his West Point classmates. She was only 14 years old but she made a serious impression on William. She was petite with a fine complexion and a lovely singing voice. Five years later, he returned to Good Springs, North Carolina and married Fanny on March 3, 1859.

After a wedding trip to Tarboro, North Carolina and Washington, D.C., they traveled to William's assignment in the Washington Territory where he was frequently absent on scouting duties. During these separations, he initiated a habit of writing to her regularly. These letters, which were full of loving sentiments, were a great solace to the teenaged bride. It was here, in the vast Northwest that Fanny gave birth to their son Samuel named after her brother.

When the war broke out William wrestled with his loyalties and found in favor of the Confederacy and North Carolina. So, the family returned to Good Springs where they remained when William left to take up his duties in the Army. He returned to his letter writing from Montgomery Alabama apologizing for having left so abruptly and urging her to be as cheerful as possible. When the two separated after two years of marriage, William was 27, Fanny 19.

Some early letters were general in nature with William discussing his military duties and often complaining that he was not receiving her mail, although she wrote often. His letters almost always included loving comments about how he missed her companionship. When she informed him that a second son was born in June, he wrote expressing his best wishes and longing to be with her during this happy event. She chose to name the child William Dorsey Jr.

In June 1861, he expressed his irritation when he learned that their new baby was to be christened but she did not tell him who the godfather was to be. His anger lingered on as he went on to say he has been dancing and flirting with a very nice girl of whom he asked a favor. Would she knit him a pouch for a lock of his wife's hair? He went on to say that the girl told him she would not work for his wife, but " . . . will do anything for me . . . "

Four days later, she replied. At the top of her letter she wrote: "Read to the End." Then she vented her fury. She asked him why he would ever write such a letter and, furthermore, why he would associate with a woman who made such "loose speech" to her husband. She went on to describe the pain he had caused her, sparing no details.

William responded with high indignation asking how she could think he would do anything dishonorable. His anger seethed throughout the letter. This highly emotional exchange seems to have cleared the air somewhat and future letters were more thoughtful and tender.

At this time, he also apologized for the letter expressing his displeasure over Dorsey's baptism, urging her to forget that he ever wrote such a letter.

Later, he wrote from Suffolk, Virginia expressed hopes that she could come and visit him there and then, abruptly, canceling this invitation since he would only be there for a short time. One can only imagine how upsetting such an indecisive letter was for Fanny.

Fanny did get to spend about three weeks with William near Smithfield, Virginia in 1861. Soon after this visit, William informed her that he was "perfectly reconciled" to being baptized and regretting that she could not be there for the ceremony.

They were reunited again in July 1862, when she visited him in Richmond followed by another get together with the children near Fredericksburg just before Lee's army moved north to Pennsylvania.

William's last letter was written from that location on the eve of the Battle of Gettysburg. It ended it with a sentimental expression of his love for her and sought for God's mercy to watch over his family adding that he hoped God would preserve them to a good old age.

William was fatally wounded at the battle of Gettysburg. In his dying moments, he asked that Fanny be told that he had no fear of dying. General Lee bemoaned the loss of one of his best men.

Fanny received the news of William's death while she was in North Caroline with their two sons and pregnant with a third. She was anticipating his return in a convalescent state. A story is told, perhaps apocryphal, that she closeted herself in her bedroom and when she emerged, the 23-year-old widow's hair had turned white.

Fanny went on to establish herself as an independent woman. She was a schoolmistress at one time and eventually was appointed postmistress of Tarboro, North Carolina. She did not remarry and died in 1922 at the age of eighty-eight. She is buried beside William in the graveyard of Calvary Church, in Tarboro.

General William Dorsey Pender was promoted to Brigadier after his gallant service at Seven Pines. Promoted to Major General in May 1863, he led his division at Gettysburg until a leg wound led to is death on July 18. When informed of Pender's death, General Lee said: "I am gradually losing my best men, Jackson, Pender, and Hood.

Bettie Mason Alexander

"I Will Try to Bear Your Absence"

A certain degree of subterfuge attended the early relationship between Bettie Mason and Porter Alexander. In the summer of 1857, Bettie was probably not aware that Porter had recently been enamored with Robert E. Lee's daughter Mary but had been rejected by her. Porter's elder sister Louisa, who tended in a loving sort of way to look after her younger sibling, had serious doubts about this new woman in his life and wrote to remind him of his recent failed affair with "Mary L." His abrupt reaction—"Who in hell is Mary L." bears testimony that his eyes had already settled on Bettie Mason.

The two lovers now faced the formidable opposition of Porter's father, the patriarchal Adam Alexander. Porter's decision to court the twenty-four year old Bettie with the intention of marrying her met with stiff opposition from the senior Alexander who was highly upset that his heir had moved ahead with this romance without informing the family. "I now care little when or whom he marries . . . he kept us in ignorance till the thing was irretrievable . . ." Porter evidently negotiated his way through these parental objections and finally asked Bettie for her hand. Later, when Adam adjusted to his son's determination, his approval was forthcoming and he eventually came to speak warmly of his new daughter-in-law.

Bettie and Porter were married on April 3, 1860 and moved to Porter's new duty assignment at the military academy at West Point. They were settling in and planning a house warming when orders arrived reassigned him to the Washington Territory. With just a week to prepare, Bettie adjusted all of her plans and the couple prepared for the month long trip through the Isthmus of Panama to the west coast. She was experiencing the exigencies of military life early in her marriage.

She admired many things about this new place: chiefly, the beautiful countryside, moderate temperatures, and friendly people. But while this rustic environment provided the men with great opportunities for hunting and fishing, she found life for the wives dull and boring. This was shortly to change in a most radical and dramatic way.

When news of succession arrived, Porter decided to resign from the U.S. Army and accept a commission in the Army of the Confederacy. Bettie was upset by this decision and seriously questioned whether other alternatives were possible. He saw none. His commander, James B. McPherson, soon to be a high-ranking Union officer, pleaded with Porter to stay loyal, to no avail. McPherson did authorize his return to New York in leave status thus allowing him to travel at Army expense.

By May 1861, Porter and Bettie were on their way home to Georgia where Bettie stayed while he went on to Richmond for his assignment.

Bettie was pregnant, with the baby expected in November. During their marriage, they were to have five children, three boys and two girls. Porter was unable to get leave and Bettie, like so many other Civil War wives, delivered Besse alone. Porter later found housing near his Virginia duty station, and they were able to be together on weekends.

Few soldiers saw more service during the war than Porter Alexander. By 1862, he had been promoted to Colonel and given command of General Longstreet's I Corps artillery. He participated in the Confederate victories at Fredericksburg and Chancellorsville and commanded the 140 cannon bombardment that preceded Pickett's charge at Gettysburg. While he was enroute as part of the invasion of Pennsylvania, Bettie wrote him sharing a dream, " . . . of your coming home & our being so happy together— but I reckon there is no such prospect in store for us, at the present at any rate . . . I will try & bear your absence without murmuring—but Oh! Ed—I want to see you so much that I sometimes think I will go crazy . . ."

When she wrote to tell him about the birth of the twins while he was away at Chattanooga, she seemed overwhelmed by the duties and responsibilities of being a single parent but still maintained a sense of humor: "I am determined to make the best of it and just give myself up entirely to baby-raising for I see no other prospect in view for me until I am over forty-five. Having three children makes me feel as if I was getting along in years. How do you feel old fellow?"

Separation also weighed heavily on Porter's mind as he longed, "for the end of the war & then Darling Bettie my own beloved wife I'll never leave you again." He anticipated, "the bright days we will have together with our children growing up around us."

Porter was wounded in the shoulder during the siege of Petersburg and was sent home to Washington, Georgia for convalescent leave. The non-life threatening nature of the wound and the presence of Bettie at his side to nurse him made this a somewhat pleasant interlude to the war.

As General Grant relentlessly pursued the war to its ultimate conclusion, Porter encouraged Bettie to bear up under the strain. He sought solace spiritually telling her that they "must look upon our separation, Darling, as a merciful dispensation to draw us closer to God . . . ."

Porter returned home after the war unannounced. It was not until Bettie heard his familiar tread on the stairs and rushed to answer the door that she realized he was home for good. The open door revealed her rushing across the room to his waiting arms.

Like so many of his fellow Confederate war veterans, Alexander was broke and needed to borrow $200 to carry them through the early post war days. This financial crisis was further complicated by the birth of another child on May 5th mandating the need to find a job quickly.

His first job offer came from the Virginia Military Institute and Bettie urged him to accept but he hesitated. Eventually he agreed to a job at the University of South Carolina as a mathematics professor and head of the department. Bette was enthusiastic, "I am delighted beyond measure to hear of the offer you had of a professor at S.C. and am exceedingly anxious for you to accept it." The salary was $1000 a year plus a house and a stipend of $50 per student.

Over the next several decades, Porter served as president of several railroads culminating with the Savannah and Memphis. Bettie, while being somewhat uneasy about the constant job shifts, was pleased that Porter was upwardly mobile and becoming financially well off. She did voice concerns about his long hours at work and scolded him about sitting up too late and smoking too many cigarettes.

Over their joint passion for hunting ducks, Porter developed a strong friendship with President Grover Cleveland. As a way of thanking Alexander for his kindness and companionship, the President offered him $1,000 a month in gold to be the U.S. boundary arbitrator between Nicaragua and Costa Rica; a job that needed to be done prior to going ahead with plans for building the Panama Canal.

This challenging job dragged on much longer than expected and kept him away from Bettie who was experiencing severe health problems. When he finally did get away from his business in Central America and sailed home, he learned on his arrival that Bettie was very ill and near death. She died one month after his return on Nov 20, 1899 and is buried in the Magnolia Cemetery in Augusta Georgia. This crippling blow was quickly followed by the equally shattering death of their daughter the following April.

Mary Mason Alexander

"The General"

In 1901, Porter married Bette's niece, Mary Mason. She was a forty-year-old spinster who wore thick glasses and became an invaluable source of help to him. She was good-natured and useful as a hostess when he was entertaining guest. He was sixty-six when they married on October 1. During their nine years of marriage, Mary referred to him as "The General." The children came to accept this marriage, but were not overly enthusiastic. She was a good companion to the aging soldier and did not take kindly to being compared to her aunt Bettie.

Edward Porter Alexander was extended the privilege of being an honored guest at the Centennial celebration at West Point on the same speakers platform with President Teddy Roosevelt. His remarks spoke of the need for unity asking, "Whose vision is now so dull that he does not realize the blessing it is to himself and to his children to live in an undivided country." The New York Times acknowledged his speech, although not devoid of controversy, to have been the best of the day.

Mary, concerned about his declining health, attempted to persuade him to stop making public appearances. But when the American Historical Association asked him to speak on Grant's role in the Battle of the Wilderness, he accepted over her strong objections. The remembrances of those in attendance noted the great respect that was extended to him but also acknowledged that he was suffering from serious memory loss and other mental problems.

Mary took him home to his South Island, Georgia retreat where he lingered on until, after several small strokes, he was brought to Savannah where he died on April 28, 1910. He is also buried at Magnolia Cemetery in Augusta, Georgia.

Mary later reminisced:

"The strife is o'er, the battle done, Alleluia!"

Brigadier General Edward Porter Alexander, a Confederate artillery officer, took part in all of the early battles of the war and gained recognition for the artillery bombardment at Gettysburg that preceded Pickett's charge. In civilian life, he was a successful businessman and author.

Libbie Bacon Custer

*"He was her *Boy General*"*

NPS Little Bighorn Battlefield

Aroused from sleep by loud knocking at the back door of her quarters at Fort Lincoln in the Dakota Territory, Libbie Custer answered in her dressing gown. She invited two officers into her parlor to hear their message, "They all died fighting at Little Big Horn!" Such news was always a possibility; her husband lived in a violent world. Although in severe shock, she immediately sent for a wrap and went to inform and console the other wives. It was her duty as the Commander's wife to do so. This tragic chapter in her young life concluded, she returned home to Monroe, Michigan.

119

The legendary Civil War hero and Indian fighter General George Armstrong Custer was gone. He perished as heroically as he had lived, and Libbie devoted her remaining years to documenting for the world her version of the "boy general."

Elizabeth Clint Bacon was born in 1842 in Monroe, Michigan to Sophia and Daniel Bacon. Her mother called her Libbie—a name she retained for the rest of her life. Three of her siblings died in infancy so from the time she was 8 years old, she was raised as an only child but her parents took great care that she was not spoiled. Sophia's childrearing philosophy centered on instilling in Libbie a concept of morality that was inner-directed instead of being determined by outside forces. Her father was well situated within Monroe society being a real estate investor, a circuit court judge as well as a Michigan state senator. Both parents wanted their daughter to be humble, modest, and religious in keeping with traditional eighteenth century values. She grew up to be a beautiful, even-tempered, intelligent, and dutiful young lady but not without occasional attempts to avoid her mother's watchful eye.

Libbie developed an early interest in keeping a diary, an activity encouraged by her father who urged her to write neatly. One notable entry was about her mother's death when she was 13 years old. These chronicles sharpened her writing skills and would prove to be most useful later in life when she set about documenting George's exploits.

After Sophia died her father sent Libbie to live with Sophia's sister and then to the Boyd Seminary, a boarding school for girls. Her mother's death had a profound impact on Libbie's life at this time. She hid her grief from others but at the same time used the sympathy offered her to her best advantage. An intelligent and dedicated student, she did well and graduated valedictorian of her class.

While attending seminary, Libbie came to the attention of many young men. Her suitors also included several older men, some of them already married. She reported an incident wherein a certain physician kissed her on New Year's Day. She promptly slapped his face. He reported it was worth it. Apparently overwhelmed by her charms, a music teacher once chased her around the piano. She was learning a great deal about men at an early age. When she was a little older, she enjoyed the attentions of a single minister and a high school principal, followed by some interest on the part of a young attorney. All were found wanting. Through all these episodes, she began to realize her potential for attracting men. During this time, Libby was an avid reader thereby cultivating the skills necessary to becoming an author in her own right, a dream she was to realize later.

George and Libbie met at a seminary party in November 1862. He was already famous for his daring exploits, which had advanced him to a position as aide to General George McClelland, then commander of the Army of the Potomac. Her initial impression of this flamboyant suitor was not favorable.

She thought his long-flowing blond hair and affectation for a cloak with a yellow lining to be ostentatious. However, after several meetings she came to blame the "God of Love" for helping her to overlook the length of his hair and making yellow her new favorite color. Love also needed to overcome her initial distaste for Army life. She had not cared for Army officers and the thought of military camp life was distasteful to her but her attraction to George forced a reevaluation. She wrote, "Every other man seems so ordinary beside my own particular star."

Her father also needed to overcome strong objections to Captain Custer, remembering him as being too fond of alcohol. His objections came to naught however, when George became a local hero and was promoted from the rank of captain to general. Father Bacon was now proud of his daughter's courtier and enjoyed the adulations that came his way as a result. But difficulty loomed that had to be overcome as well. George had been encouraged by Libbie to see other women, a ploy designed to control local gossip about their evolving relationship. One of his "other women" was a girl named Fanny who had attracted George's attention. Once Libbie decided that George was to be her man, she made it clear that the "other women" needed to disappear. George complied. The lovers were separated when George was sent back to the front, but Libbie maintained a regular correspondence that insured the relationship would continue to thrive.

In December, George wrote his sister that he was marrying Libbie in February. He was confident that she would approve and that Libbie would be coming to visit her shortly.

On February 9, 1864 George and Libbie were married with hundreds in attendance. It was the gala social activity of the year. Three hundred guests attended the reception. The new bride was the sparkling presiding spirit over the affair, greeting everyone lively exuberance.

The wedding trip included visits to Cleveland, Buffalo, New York, Washington, and finally, on to his duty post on the Rapidan River in Virginia. The honeymoon also included a visit with General George McClellan and his wife Ellen. Libbie remembered being impressed by Ellen's grace and vibrant personality and by her husband's willingness to help Ellen with words when she had difficulty hearing. (Apparently she suffered from a hearing loss.)

Libbie experienced a shocking transition to military life. Her indoctrination included George's advice to avoid housework, not to criticize other officers, and to keep her political opinions to herself. She could dance, ride, and walk with whomever she wanted, but was never to single out any one officer to become in any way a special favorite. When receiving company, she was to treat everyone alike. When Libbie once protested that she found it difficult being nice to someone she did not consider to be lady-like, George replied that the lady was an officer's wife and as a guest, was to be treated as such.

Living in tents or as a guest in strange houses required much forbearance on Libbie's part. But as a loyal wife she tried to stay close to the Army during the last year of the war. When the occasion called for it, Libbie was to demonstrate both courage and clear—headedness. During a flash flood, many wagons were washed away and several men drowned. Libbie and her maid Lesa jumped to the aid of several soldiers by throwing them life saving ropes and then tending to the survivors. Custer's cavalry duties often required being called away on short notice and Libbie preferred to stay in Washington when he was away. She remained ready to respond to any reasonable request from George to join him during the last hectic year of the war. Military life did have its compensations. She enjoyed the six course meals that Union cavalry commander General Alfred Pleasonton hosted and wrote her father about the style and privileges she enjoyed as a general's wife.

In her married life she continued to have difficulties fending off the advances of other men. Aware that the influence of powerful men in Congress might help George, she had to strike a delicate balance when several of them thought her to be quite attractive and desirable. Several senators actively sought her attention, but she was able to avoid their advances without insulting them. She seemed to delight in telling George the details of each encounter. She knew that her spouse was known for his roving eye toward the opposite sex thereby making flirtatious behavior on her part permissible. She seemed to equivocate on the subject, however, when she wrote that although she had a pretty face, it was her dashing husband's reputation that brought her to the attention of other men.

Libbie once met President Abraham Lincoln at a reception. After she shook his hand and moved on he suddenly made the connection with the name Custer and grabbed her hand again saying, "So this is the young woman whose husband goes into a charge with a whoop and a shout . . ." As she left she asked one of his secretaries to tell Mr. Lincoln he would have gained a vote if soldiers' wives were allowed the privilege. Libbie always had a soft spot in her heart for Union cavalry hero General Philip Sheridan, George's commanding officer, who impressed her by his considerate concern on her behalf. She even named her horse Phil Sheridan. At Winchester he ordered all wives to leave but made an exception for Libbie. After the Confederate surrender at Appomattox, Sheridan purchased the table upon which General Grant wrote the surrender terms and gave it to Libbie with this note:

"My Dear Madam,

I respectfully present to you this small writing table on which the conditions for the surrender of the Confederate Army of Northern Virginia were written by Lt. General Grant, and permit me to say, Madam, that there is scarcely an individual in our service who has contributed more to bring this about than your very gallant husband."

Libbie's post war experience included going west with George when he was assigned duty securing the frontier against Indian attacks. He had accepted the rank of Lt. Colonel in 1866 in order to serve in the regular, post Civil War Army. She dealt with rattlesnakes, dust storms, extended periods of boredom, meager amenities, cold and crude housing, and the ever-present danger of Indian attacks with courage and fortitude. A correspondent from the *New York World* wrote of Libbie after visiting Fort Lincoln, " . . . a charming lady, who has shared marches and victories . . . is a green spot, if there be no others, in the frontier life of the officers . . ."

The Custers were so fond of dogs that at one time they owned 80 hounds. They hired a private who said it was his job to keep the difficulties associated with the dogs from bothering George. He fed them and paid off irate farmers when the dogs attacked their livestock.

The next 10 years were troublesome for Libbie. George was known to have had at least three extramarital affairs that caused Libbie considerable grief. He had also turned to gambling very heavily. When faced with her wrath however, he was always able to turn on his considerable charm, expounding to her how poorly these other women faired in comparison to her.

After George Armstrong Custer rode into American history at the Battle of Little Big Horn, Libbie had to face life without him. Grieving over her loss, Libbie turned to her cousin and good friend Rebecca Richmond who urged her to accept the mantle of her heroic husband, "Wear it Libbie, for his sake!" she urged. Rebecca's advice resounded deeply and Libbie soon became committed to her hero's memory. When she found that George had planned to honor the family debt with what little money he had left her, she realized she needed to make a living for herself in a male-dominated world. Finding another man was not an option.

Libbie did not like the statue erected at George's gravesite at West Point depicting a cavalryman charging with a sword in one hand and a pistol in the other. She considered the memorial grotesque and a dishonor to her fallen hero. She recalled that she literally cried the statue off its pedestal. It was eventually replaced with one more to her liking.

Libbie became almost obsessed with telling the story of her "boy general" with such vehemence that no reasonable reader could ever doubt his loyalty, bravery, and military skills. She wrote three popular books about him (*Boots and Saddles, Tenting on the Plains,* and *Following the Guidon.)*

She also became a celebrity on the lecture circuit, often delivering spellbinding renditions of her lover's heroics and her experiences on the Western frontier. Since she made lucrative investments with her money, she was able to live a comfortable life and enjoyed a prestigious New York address on Park Avenue. Her success allowed her to leave a legacy of over $113,000 dollars when she died in 1933. Libbie's generosity included a contribution of $5,000 to a scholarship trust at Vassar College that continues to provide scholarships today.

Historians consider the enthusiastic and adulatory nature of her writings as being central to the continuing myth of General Custer, his dramatic life and fiery ending at Little Big Horn. Modern literary criticism has placed her writings into a more realistic perspective without diminishing his considerable reputation as a true American hero. During her active writing years, Union Generals Grant, Sherman, and Sheridan were staunch supporters of their flamboyant subordinate and extended extraordinary courtesies to Libbie in her efforts to document Custer's reputation.

Libbie and George are buried side by side at the United States Military Academy at West Point.

She was grateful to have lived to hear President Theodore Roosevelt describe her husband as "a shining light to all the youth of America." Her mission had been accomplished!

Major General George Custer was one of the most celebrated figures to emerge from the War. He fought with distinction in the cavalry battles of the Army of the Potomac. It was his army service after the war that caused his reputation to suffer and he died at the battle of Little Big Horn on June 25, 1876.

The Three Wives of General George Pickett

Twice married and twice a much grieved widower, George Pickett was 38 when he married Sallie Corbell in 1863 and was finally able to achieve some brief, albeit troubled, marital longevity. It was Sallie that was to champion his cause after his death and sought through her writings to elevate "Her Soldier" to Civil War immortality. General Robert E. Lee's fateful words as he looked out at Gettysburg's Cemetery Ridge on July 3rd 1863—"the enemy is there and I am going to strike him"—sealed George Pickett's fate as one of the most ill fated and star-crossed warriors of the Civil War. Although of the roughly 12,000 confederate soldiers involved in the gallant but futile attack, less than 6,000 were under Pickett's direct command, history would forever document the failed event as "Pickett's Charge".

Sally Harrison Minge

First Love

When Sally Harrison Minge met George Pickett he was an established Mexican War hero with charming and gallant ways towards women. Before long she was completely under his spell and agreed to marry him. Coming from Virginia's upper crust society, Sally and George seemed well suited for one another. However, her parents, Dr. John and Mary Minge, had serious concerns about how their daughter, used to the finer things in life, would adjust to army life on the Texas frontier.

Twenty-one year old Sally married twenty-six year old George in January, 1851 and after a wedding trip to New Orleans, the newlyweds traveled to Fort Gates, Texas, about fifty miles southwest of Austin, the closest town. By this time Sally was three months pregnant. All thoughts of adventurous army life quickly evaporated under the reality of living in primitive, inadequate quarters plagued by extreme heat, vermin, and fine dust that permeated everywhere. Faced with this hostile environment, Sally sought to cope with her coming confinement as bravely as she could without any of the refinements that normally attended the childbearing process.

On November 13, 1851 she gave birth to a girl; however, neither mother nor child survived. George took their bodies back to Virginia where he took a long leave hoping to cope with his deep mourning.

According to the last Mrs. Pickett, Sallie, it was during this time that she came upon the bereaved widowed soldier while walking along the seashore near Old Point Comfort. She was nine years old when this encounter occurred and understanding his great sorrow, offered him her juvenile compassion. As she later described the meeting, "He drew me to him telling me that he had lost his wife Sally and his little girl, and that he was very lonely. I asked him their names; they both had been called Sally. You can call me Sally, I'll be your wife and little girl," I replied. "That's a promise," he said, "You shall be named Sally and be my wife." She replied that she would call him "Her Soldier," a term she was later to use throughout her writings about him.

Since there are no corroborating sources to this romantic rendezvous, historians dismiss the notion that there was any discussion of marriage at this meeting, rather attributing this dialogue to the highly emotional and romantic style that was to characterize much of Sallie's later writings.

Morning Mist

The Indian Maid

George went back to duty in Texas and was soon transferred to Fort Vancouver in the Oregon territory. His duties there required him to negotiate with the local Indian tribe. He succeeded in learning their language and thereby earn their trust. He soon met a Haida native called Sakis Tiigang; also know by the more poetic name of Morning Mist. She was the beautiful daughter of the local chieftain or tribal leader. In 1857, they were married in both an Indian and a civil ceremony. She moved into his house on Bancroft Street in Bellingham, Washington. (The house still stands and is maintained by the Washington State Historical Society) Some time later, while giving birth to a son, she suffered greatly. George's army surgeon was summoned, but arrived too late to save her. Their son, named James, survived.

By1859, George, considering the difficulties of raising a young child on his own, placed him in adoption with a childless couple named Catherine and William Collins. When the Civil War broke out and George went east to join the Confederate army, he gave the Collins's $100 to assist with James's care. Later, James demonstrated artistic talents and his new parents sent him to art school in San Francisco. He was an excellent student and went on to become an accomplished artist. There is no record that George ever made contact with his son and would never see him again.

Sallie Ann Corbell

"Cupid Does Not Readily Give Way to Mars"

LaSalle from What Happend To me

George's third wife was born Sallie Ann Corbell on May 16,1843 to John David and Elizabeth Phillips Corbell. By 1861, Sallie was in her late teens and had grown to be a physically attractive and intellectually accomplished young lady. George was stationed with the Confederate army in Virginia; about 15 miles from the Corbell home in Chuckatuck, Virginia. He took full advantage of this proximity and their courtship was characterized by the frequency with which he absented himself from duty to go courting Sallie, much to the irritation of his fellow officers. Reports are that he would leave late at night and return early in the morning so as not to be missed. Sallie later claimed that he made the thirty mile round trip almost every night.

"Cupid does not readily give way to Mars," Sallie explained in her autobiography, "and in our Southern country, a lull between bugle calls was likely to be filled with the music of wedding bells." During such a lull, George and Sallie were married at Richmond in September of 1863; she was 15, he, 38. Jefferson and Varina Davis and Mary Custis Lee were in attendance along with many other dignitaries. Sallie exclaimed she felt like a child "who had been given a bunch of grapes, a stick of candy. Oh, I was happy."

During the summer of 1864, Sallie gave birth to their first child, George Jr., her "new little soldier." The child was a great favorite among Pickett's troops during Sallie's frequent visits to camp. She later described one incident when she accompanied her husband as he inspected the front lines thereby exposing her to exploding shells. Pickett pleaded with her to leave. "'No indeed,' I said. 'I'm not a bit afraid, and if I were do you think I would let Pickett's men see me run?"

In the aftermath of the terrific loss his division suffered at Gettysburg, life was becoming increasingly difficult for George. His health was poor and he also drank excessively. Sources also indicated that he was rapidly loosing his appetite for war and several officers blamed Sallie for his lack of focus and seemingly cowardly behavior on the battlefield. His absence when the Union attacked his position during the Battle of Sayler's Creek resulted in his dismissal from the army by General Lee who noted that Pickett's men were unsoldierly, lax in discipline, and loose in military instruction.

Unlike many Civil war veterans who greeted peace with gratitude and looked forward to resuming some semblance of a normal life, George and Sallie continued to be plagued with troubles. Like other southern soldiers, the Picketts had invested all their money in Confederate bonds which now proved worthless and George's childhood home at Turkey Island was in ashes. Their plight was further exacerbated by the disturbing discovery that the federal government was about to press war crime charges on the ex-general. This accusation related back to Pickett's duties as a wartime appointment to the Department of North Carolina in 1863. In this role, he had ordered the court-martial and execution of twenty-two North Carolinians accused of treason. Union official were outraged and demanded an explanation. Facing this indictment, he fled to Canada in disguise. Sallie and the baby soon followed. They stayed in Montreal for approximately six weeks. Sallie later claimed these weeks in Canada were the happiest times of her life. Her writings never mentioned the war crimes charges.

Since the government never did file formal charges against George, he decided to return to the states and ask General Grant for a pardon. Instead of a pardon Grant offered him an endorsement that permitted him to travel in the states without being further charged. George and Sallie tried to farm his father's land, but were unsuccessful. In the process, they both suffered severely from over exertion. He experienced great guilt over his failure to provide for her as a proper southern husband. Sallie herself held up well during this hardship considering that she was not used to hard labor. He finally made a little money selling insurance, but they never recovered the prosperous life they had both had enjoyed during the antebellum years. A bitter disillusioned man, George Pickett died in 1875 at age 53.

Sallie had saved over 40 wartime letters from George and decided to use them to tell his story. She noted that some ex-Confederate officers were blaming one another for the loss of the war and she was not going to let any unwarranted criticism fall on her husband. She took many noticeable liberties with the facts and the historian is left to seriously question several of her conclusions—some even accusing her of outright mendacity and forgery. However, she was not alone in embellishing her wartime remembrances but joined several ex-soldiers who also took liberties with the facts in retelling their martial experiences. Aware of these practices, Sallie had no compunctions in presenting George in the best possible light.

She went on to author several books. It was during this period of her life that she used the name LaSalle Pickett. This change of name confuses many who assume that LaSalle was her name all along. *Pickett and His Men* and *Heart of a Soldier* received much favorable attention and helped Sallie's financial difficulties. While historians observe that she did not always get her battlefield facts straight, veterans loved the books and the author. She prepared a series of articles for Cosmopolitan Magazine in commemoration of the fiftieth anniversary of the Battle of Gettysburg that were well received especially by the veterans of Pickett's command. When she appeared at the Gettysburg reunion of 1887, the New York Times claimed that she was the center of attraction for both northern and southern veterans. She had not only written and lectured extensively, but she was a charming southern lady as well as Pickett's widow. At one time she was the guest of Union war hero Lawrence Chamberlain at his home in Maine who also professed to be charmed.

Eventually, however, the grieving war widow image lost its luster and her financial situation worsened. She also encountered several episodes of very poor health. To add to her woes in 1911, her son, George Jr. died of yellow fever while serving as a U.S. Army major in the Philippines.

One of Sallie's more fanciful stories involves no less a hero of the War than the President of the United States himself. Shortly after the Confederates had abandoned Richmond, Lincoln did in fact visit the city. Sallie claimed that during this visit, Lincoln knocked on her door and introduced himself as, "Abraham Lincoln, George's old friend." She said he had then held her baby saying, "Tell your Father I forgive him." The improbable act of a benevolent president—or further evidence of the imaginative fancies of a loving wife?

Sallie, who survived her husband by 56 years, died in 1931 and was buried in Arlington National Cemetery. 67 years later in 1998, she was disinterred and is now buried, in accord with her dying wish, next to "Her Soldier" in Richmond's Hollywood Cemetery.

Major General George Pickett, served with distinction during the Seven Days' Campaign, was wounded at Gaines Mill, fought at Fredericksburg and, of course, led his division in what was to become known as Pickett's Charge at Gettysburg. After the war he and his family fled to Canada to avoid arrest on war crime charges. They returned when General Grant offered him safe passage.

Irene Rucker Sheridan

"Great Cavalry Leader Vanquished by a Blond"

This wife of a Civil War general married her general after the war.

Irene Rucker was the daughter of General Daniel H. Rucker, the assistant quartermaster for the U.S. Army. Born on an Army reservation in Fort Union, New Mexico in 1855. She lived in Army circles all of her life and was aware of the vital role General Sheridan had played in the Civil War.

Philip Sheridan was born in 1831 to Irish immigrants parents. His father was a moderately successful businessman and his mother was a pillar in the local Catholic Church.

Irene met her future husband at a wedding in 1874. Philip courted her with increasing seriousness from that day on. This caused some sensation when the pretty "Miss Rucker" and the famous general were seen riding on the Chicago streets in an open carriage. In was a common assumption that Philip was a confirmed bachelor dedicated to his profession with little time for woman. His conscientious pursuit of Irene Rucker was a surprise to his friends and a source of disappointment to several ladies who thought he would make a rich and distinguished husband.

She was half his age when they were married on June 3, 1875 at the Tucker House in Chicago. Neither viewed the age difference as a problem. Philip's friend, General William Sherman, was delighted with the match and even expressed some envy—an observation that did not please Mrs. Sherman.

In deference to the recent death of his father, the wedding was a low-key event. Five others generals attended, including Sherman and John Pope. The Chicago paper ran a headline, "Great Cavalry Leader Vanquished by a Blonde." Sheridan thought that was hilarious and roared with laughter. To him, Irene was more than just a "blonde"; she was well educated, attractive, and poised for her age.

The honeymoon, planned as a three-month tour of he Pacific Northwest, was cut short when a Sioux uprising required the grooms recall to duty.

The new bride anticipated she might need to subtly coax Philip to change his bachelor ways. She knew he enjoyed attending the races and spend time at his men's clubs, and she wondered if his old habits would interfere with her ideas of family life. Philip proved to be a quick study and easily adapted to the smooth way Irene came into her own as a hostess entertaining his important friends with style and dignity. Philip was impressed with her tendency to think before she spoke and if she had nothing constructive to say, remain silent.

They first lived in Chicago, but his Army assignment took them to Washington, D. C. where they lived in a large house on Rhode Island Avenue, a gift from Chicago friends who were grateful for his support following the Chicago fire of 1871.

The Sheridan's had four children: Mary in 1876, twin girls, Louse and Irene in 1877, and Phil in 1880. Phillip surprised many when he displayed an avid interest in fatherhood and doted on his children. Irene matured from the 'pretty Miss Rucker' to the 'lovely Mrs. Sheridan.'

By 1887, Philips health had deteriorated and Irene decided to have him moved from Washington to a shore cottage in Nonquitt, Massachusetts. Shortly thereafter, Philip suffered a heart attack and became bedridden. Congress had voted him a fourth star shortly before he died, an act that pleased him greatly.

With Irene at his bedside, he died on August 5, 1887, the day after he had approved the galleys for his memoirs. President Grover Cleveland led the funeral cortege of 1500 mourners to Saint Matthews's church in Washington.

Irene never remarried declaring, "I would rather be the widow of Phil Sheridan than the wife of any living man." Thus, she remained single as did her three daughters. As a family, they moved to 2551 Massachusetts Avenue in 1908 in order to be near the statue erected to honor husband and father at Sheridan Square. The story goes that the four of them would lean out their bedroom window each morning greeting their fallen warrior, "Good morning Papa."

Philip's death left them comfortable financially with houses in Washington and Chicago.

Irene died at age 83.

General Philip Henry Sheridan is known as one of three Union generals who won the greatest fame in the Civil War. His success in the Valley in 1864 made him a household name n the North. He followed Grant and Sherman as Commanding General of the Army in 1884.

References alphabetical

Betty Mason and Mary Mason Alexander   115

- Gallagher, Gary W., Editor, *Fighting for the Confederacy, The Personal Reflections of General Edward Porter Alexander,* University of North Carolina Press, Chapel Hill, 1989.
- Golay, Michael, *To Gettysburg and Beyond: The Parallel lives of Joshua Chamberlain and Edward Porter Alexander,* Sarpedon, 2000.
- Klein, Maury, *Edward Porter Alexander,* University of Georgia Press, Athens, Georgia, 1971.
- Web site
    us-civilar.com/Alexander

Eliza Clinch Anderson   19

- Garrison, Webb, *Amazing Women of the Civil War,* Rutledge Hill Press, Nashville, Tennessee, 1999.
- Waugh, John G., *Class of 1846,* Warner Books, Inc, N.Y., 1994.
- Web sites:
    tulane.edu/~latner/Anderson/
    www.picturehistory.com/find/p3781/mcms.html

Arabella Griffith Barlow   30

- Conklin, Eileen F. *Women at Gettysburg, 1863,* Thomas Publications, 1993.
- Welch, Richard F., *The Boy General,* Rosemont Publishing & Printing, Danvers, Mass., 2003.
- Web sites:
    http://freepages.genealogy.rootsweb.com/~barlow/francis.htm#
    http://famous Americans.net

Fanny Adams Chamberlain 39

- Longacre, Edward, *Joshua Chamberlain—The Soldier and the Man*, Combined Publishing, Conshohocken, PA., 1999.
- Pullen, John, *Joshua Chamberlain,* John Pullen, Stackpole Books, 1999
- Smith, Jennifer, I. "The Reconstruction of 'Home'", in Carol K. Blesser and Lesley J. Gordon, *Intimate Strategies of the Civil War,* Oxford University Press, New York, 2001.

Libby Bacon Custer 119

- Arruda, Suzanne, *Libbie: The Girl He Left Behind*, Avisson Press, Greenboro, North Carolina Custer, Elizabeth, *Boots and Saddles*, University of Oklahoma Press, Norman, Oklahoma,1975.
- Merington, Marguerite, ed. *The Custer Story*, University of Oklahoma Press, 1965.
- Leckie, Shirley, *Elizabeth Bacon Custer and the Making of a Myth*, University of Oklahoma Press, 1993.
- Leckie, Shirley, "The Civil War Partnership of Elizabeth and George A. Custer" Carol K. Blesser and Lesley J. Gordon, *Intimate Strategies of the Civil War,* Oxford University Press, New York, 2001.
- Longacre, Edward, "Alfred Pleasanton," Civil War Times, December, 1974.
- Reynolds, Arlene, *The Civil War Memories of Elizabeth Bacon Custer*, University of Texas Press,1994.
- Web site
    http://famousamericans.net

Lizinka Cambell Ewell 22

- Carmichael Peter, S. "All Say They Are Under Petticoat Government", in Carol K. Blesser and Lesley J. Gordon, *Intimate Strategies of the Civil War,* Oxford University Press, New York, 2001.
- Casdorph, Paul D., *Confederate General R. S. Ewell*, University Press of Kentucky, 2004.
- Pfantz, Donald C., *Richard S. Ewell, A Soldiers Life.* University of North Carolina Press, Chapel Hill, North Carolina, 1998.

Mary Montgomery Forrest 44

- Henry, Robert Selph, *"First With the Most Forrest,"* Greenwood Press, Westport, Connecticut, 1974.
- Wyeth, John Allen, *That Devil Forest*, Louisiana State University Press, Baton Rouge, Louisiana, 1959.

Jesse Benton Fremont 33

- Herr, Pamela, *Jessie Benton Fremont*, University of Oklahoma Press, Norman, Oklahoma,1987.

- Herr, Pamela, "Permutations of a Marriage", in Carol K. Blesser and Lesley J. Gordon, *Intimate Strategies of the Civil War*, Oxford University Press, New York, 2001.
- Nevins, Allen, *Fremont: Pathfinder of the West*, Frederick Ungar, New York, 1966. Parrish, William E., "Fremont in Missouri," *Civil War Times*, April 1978.
- Websites
    http://www.ohiocivilwar.com/fremont.html (Fremont Body Guard)
    http://www.fulcrum-resources.com/hmtl/women

Fanny Haralson Gordon   106
- Conklin, Eileen F., *Woman at Gettysburg*, Thomas Publications, Gettysburg, Pa. 1993.
- Eckert, Ralph Lowell, *John Brown Gordon*, Louisiana State University Press, Baton Rouge, Louisiana, 1989.
- Goins, Craddock, *The Bride of the Gray Chevalier*, The Magazine of the South, February, 1983.
- Gordon, John Brown, *Reminiscences of the Civil War*, Morningside Press, Dayton, Ohio, 1903 and 1993.
- Hargrett Rare Book and Manuscript Library, University of Georgia, Athens Georgia.
    o   Atlanta Journal, April 28, 1931
    o   Augusta Herald, April 28, 1931
    o   Augusta Herald, May 29, 1931
    o   Gordon, Caroline Lewis, *De Gin'ral an' Miss Fanny*, unpublished manuscript,1904.
    o   Gordon, John B. letter dated May 10, 1863.
    o   Gordon, Fanny, letter dated May 10,1872.
    o   Lee, Robert E., letter dated February 25, 1872.
- Tankersley, Allen, *"Mrs. John B. Gordon, Heroine of the Confederacy"*, The United Daughters of the Confederacy Magazine, Richmond, Virginia, May 1952.

Julia Dent Grant   47
- Simon, John,Y., "A Marriage Tested by War", in Carol K. Blesser and Lesley J. Gordon, *Intimate Strategies of the Civil War*, Oxford University Press, New York, 2001.
- Grant, Julia Dent, *Personal Memoirs*, Southern Illinois University Press, 1975.
- Longstreet, James, *From Manassas To Appomattox*, Indiana University Press, Bloomington, Indiana, 1960.
- Perry, Mark, *Grant and Twain*, Random House, 2004.
- Ross, Isabel, *The General's Wife*, Dodd, Mead, New York, 1959.

- Simpson, Brooks D., *Ulysses S. Grant*, Houghton Mifflin Co., Boston, Massachusetts, 2000.
- Websites
  http://www.lkwdpl.org/wihohio/gran-jul.htm
  *http://explore.org/index.php?id=210*http://*www.whitehouse.gov/history/firstladies*

Almira Russell Hancock 80
- Hancock, Almira R., *Reminiscences of Winfield Scott Hancock*, Paperback Edition, Digital Scanning, New York, 1887, 2001.
- Jordan, David M., *Winfield Scott Hancock—A Soldier's Life*, Indiana University Press, Bloomington, Indiana,1996.

Lucy Webb Hayes 73
- Garrison, Webb, "Lucy Hayes, Scout", *Amazing Women of the Civil War*, Rutledge Press, Nashville, Tennessee, 1999.
- Geer, Emily A., *First Lady*, Kent State University Press, 1984.
- Web sites:
  www.epworth.com/cameo2.htm
  www.usatrivia.com/flbihay.htm
  www.whitehouse.gov/history/firstladies

Katherine Hewitt 78
- Longacre, Edward G., *John F. Reynolds*, Civil War Times Aug 72. Nichols, Edward, J., *Toward Gettysburg*, Pennsylvania State University Press, University Park, Pennsylvania, 1958.
- Website
  www.emmitsburg.net/archive_list/articles/civil_war/doc_civil_war.htm

Kitty Morgan Hill 89
- Robertson, James, *General A. P. Hill: The Story of a Confederate Warrior*, Vintage, 1992.
- Website
  www.aphilesa.com/family.html

Elinor Junkin and Mary Anna Morrison Jackson 84
- Bowers, John, *Stonewall Jackson*, Morrow, New York, 1989.
- Jackson, May Anna, *Life and Letters of Stonewall Jackson*, Harper & Brothers, 1892.
- Jackson, Mary Anna, *Memoirs of Stonewall Jackson*, Morningside Bookshop, Dayton, Ohio, 1993.

- O'.Brien, Jean Getman, *The Last Days of Jackson*, Civil War Times, December, 1963.
- Riter, Ben, *The Widow's Favorite*, Civil War Times, February,1979.
- Website
  www.vmi.edu/archives/jackson

Mary Custis Lee   13
- Andrews, Matthew, *"Appomattox As Viewed by Mrs. R. L. Lee,"* Virginia Historical Society Connelly, Thomas, L., *The Marble Man*, Louisiana State University Press, Baton Rouge, 1977.
- Perry, John, *Mrs. Robert E. Lee*, Multonomah Publishers, 2001.
- Taylor, John, *Duty Faithfully Performed*, Brassey's, 1999.
- Website
  civilwarhistory.com/custis.htm

Louise Garland and Helen Dortch Longstreet   56
- DiNardo, R.L. & Nofi, Albert A. editors, *James Longstreet*, Combines Publishing, Conshohocken, Pennsylvania, 1998.
- Life Magazine, December 27, 1943.
- Piston, William G., *Lee's Tarnished Lieutenant*, University of Georgia Press, Athens, Georgia, 1987.
- Simpson, Brooks D., *Ulysses S. Grant*, Houghton Mifflin Co., Boston, Massachusetts, 2000.
- Wert, Jeffry D., *General James Longstreet*, Touchstone, New York, E-mail correspondence with Dan Paterson, Feb. 16, 2005

Mary Ellen Marcy McClellan   92
- Myers, William S, *General George Brinton McClellan*, D. Appleton-Century, 1934.
- Sears, Stephen W., *George B. McClellan—The Little Napoleon*, Ticknor & Fields, 1988.
- Waugh, John C., *Class of 1846*, Warner Books, New York, 1994.

Margaretta Sergeant Meade   27
- Cleave, Freeman, *Meade of Gettysburg*, University of Oklahoma Press, Norman, Oklahoma,1960.
- Meade, George, *The Life and Letters of George Gordon Meade*, Stan Clark Military Books, 1996.
- Tagg, Larry, *The Generals of Gettysburg*, Savas Publishing, 'Eldorado Hills, California,1998.

Fanny Sheppard Pender   112

- Hassler, William W., editor, *One of Lee's Best Men*, The University of North Carolina Press, Chapel Hill, North Carolina, 1965.

Sallie (LaSalle) Corbell Pickett   128

- Boltz, Martha M., *The General's Second Family*, The Washington Times, Washington D.C., 2001.
- Edson, Lelah Jackson, *The Fourth Corner*, Craftsman Press, Seattle Washington, 1968.
- George E. Pickett: *Virginia's Premier Gamecock,* Knight Templer, August and September, 1998.
- Gordon, Lesley, J., "Cupid Does Not Readily Give Way to Mars", in Carol K. Blesser and Lesley J. Gordon, *Intimate Strategies of the Civil War,* Oxford University Press, New York, 2001.
- Jesley J. Gordon, *George E Pickett in Life and Legend,* University of North Carolina Press, Chapel Hill, North Carolina, 1998.
- Longacre, Edward, *Joshua Chamberlain,* Combined Publishing, Pennsylvania, 1999.
- Longstreet James, *From Manassas To Appomattox*, Indiana University Press, Bloomington, Indiana, 1960.
- Pickett, LaSalle, *Pickett and His Men,* Foote & Davis, 1899.
- Pickett, LaSalle, *The Heart of a Soldier*, Stan Clark Military Books, Gettysburg, Pennsylvania, 1913 reprinted 1995.
- Reardon, Carol, *Pickett's Charge in History and Memory*, University of North Carolina Press, Chapel Hill, North Carolina, 1997.
- Waugh, John, C., *The Class of 1846,* Warner Books, New York, 1994.
- Website
  www.pickettsociety.com

Ellen Ewing Sherman   66

- Barrett, John G., *Sherman's March Through the Carolinas,* University of North Carolina Press, Chapel Hill, North Carolina, 1956.
- Hart, B. H. Liddell, *Sherman*, Frederick A. Praeger, New York, 1958.
- Kennett, Lee, *Sherman: A Soldier's Life*, Harper Collins, New York, 2001.
- Lewis, Lloyd, *Sherman: Fighting Prophet,* University of Nebraska Press, Reprint Edition, Lincoln, Nebraska, 1993.
- Marszalek, John, F. "A Contentious Union", in Carol K. Blesser and Lesley J. Gordon, *Intimate Strategies of the Civil War,* Oxford University Press, New York, 2001.
- Massey, Mary Elizabeth, *Women in the Civil War,* University of Nebraska Press, Lincoln, Nebraska, 1966.
- Sherman, William T., *William Tecumseh Sherman*, Library of America, New York, 1984.

Teresa Baglioli Sickles 97

- Brandt, Nat, *The Congressman Who Got Away With Murder*, Syracuse University Press, 1991.
- Keneally, Thomas, *American Scoundrel*, Random House, New York, 2002.
- Swansberg, W. A., *Sickles the Incredible*, Charles Scribner's Sons, 1984. "In 1859, Capital Was a Wild, Wild Washington" by Sarah Mark, July 17, 2000, *Washington Post* "Warning to Seducers" *Frank Leslie's Illustrated Newspaper*, Saturday, April 9, 1859.
- Websites
  www.assumption.edu/dept/history/Hill3net/sickles/default1.html
  www.assumption.edu/users/McClymer/his260/Sickles Notes.html
  http://www.assumption.edu/acad/ii/Academic/history/Hi113net/sickles/ default2.html

Irene Rucker Sheridan 131

- Morris, Roy Jr., *Sheridan,* Vintage Books, NY 1993
- Web site:
  www.arlington.net/ireneuc

Flora Cook Stuart 102

- Davis, Burke, *Jeb Stuart: The Last Cavalier,* Wings Books, New York, 1957.
- McClellan, Henry B., *I Rode With Jeb Stuart*, Indiana University Press, Bloomington, Indiana,1958
- Nesbitt, Mark, *Saber and Scapegoat,* Stackpole Books, Mechanicsburg, Pennsylvania, 1994.
- Thompson, John W, *Jeb Stuart*, C. Scribners, New York, 1958.

Susan Tarleton 53

- Cantor, George, *Confederate Generals,* Taylor Trade Publications, Dallas, Texas, 2000.
- Purdue, Howell & Elizabeth, *Pat Cleburne, Confederate General*, College Press, Hillsboro, Texas, 1973.
- Symonds, Craig L., *Stonewall of the West*, University of Kansas Press, Manhattan, Kansas, 1997.
- From web site
  http://www.springhillandfranklin.com/4/2

Susan Elston Wallace 62

- Hanson, Victor, *Ripples of Battles,* Anchor Books, 2003 Benson J. Lossing Collection, Huntington Library, San Marino, California, 2003.
- McKee, Irving, *Ben-Hur Wallace*, University of California Press, Berkeley, California, 1947.

- Swift, Glroia, "Honor Redeemed: Lew Wallace," *North and South*, January 2001.
- Wallace, Lew, *An Autobiography*, Harper Brothers, New York, 1906
- Website
    bbs.keyhole.com.
- National Park Service web site,
    - o Robert Spude, "Exploring Hispanic History & Culture"
    - o Lew Wallace, Author of Ben Hur, bbs.keyhole.com
    - o General Wallace Study and Museum, letter to Susan, 3 March 1885, ben-hur.com

Printed in the United States
52315LVS00003B/89

9 781425 704971